endorsed for

edexcel

Edexcel GCSE

History B

Schools History Project

Medicine and Surgery

Authors:

Cathy Warren

Nigel Bushnell

Series Editor:

Angela Leonard

Updated for the
2013 specifications by:

Rob Bircher

Kirsty Taylor

ALWAYS LEARNING

PEARSON

Published by Pearson Education Limited, Edinburgh Gate, Harlow, Essex, CM20 2JE.

www.pearsonschoolsandfecolleges.co.uk

Copies of official specifications for all Edexcel qualifications may be found on the Edexcel website: www.edexcel.com

Text © Pearson Education Limited 2013
Typeset & Illustrated by www.hlstudios.eu.com
Original illustrations © Pearson Education Limited 2009
Cover photo/illustration © Corbis/Bettmann

The rights of Cathy Warren, Nigel Bushnell, Rob Bircher and Kirsty Taylor to be identified as authors of this work have been asserted by them in accordance with the Copyright, Designs and Patents Act 1988.

First published 2013

16 15 14 13
10 9 8 7 6 5 4 3 2 1

British Library Cataloguing in Publication Data
A catalogue record for this book is available from the British Library

ISBN 978 1 44690 680 4

Printed by Neografia

A note from the publisher
In order to ensure that this student book offers high-quality support for the associated Edexcel qualification, it has been through a review process by the awarding organisation to confirm that it fully covers the teaching and learning content of the specification or part of a specification at which it is aimed, and demonstrates an appropriate balance between the development of subject skills, knowledge and understanding, in addition to preparation for assessment.

While the publishers have made every attempt to ensure that advice on the qualification and its assessment is accurate, the official specification and associated assessment guidance materials are the only authoritative source of information and should always be referred to for definitive guidance.

Edexcel examiners have not contributed to any updated sections in this resource relevant to examination papers for which they have responsibility.

No material from an endorsed student book will be used verbatim in any assessment set by Edexcel.

Endorsement of a student book does not mean that the student book is required to achieve this Edexcel qualification, nor does it mean that it is the only suitable material available to support the qualification, and any resource lists produced by the awarding organisation shall include this and other appropriate resources.

Edexcel GCSE History B Schools History Project: Medicine (1A) and Surgery (3A) SB 2013

Acknowledgements

The author and publisher would like to thank the following individuals and organisations for permission to reproduce photographs: (Key: b-bottom; c-centre; l-left; r-right; t-top)

akg-images Ltd: 23, 34, 36 (Housewife), 48l; **Alamy Images:** Inspire Stock Inc. 9 (Obstetrician), Janine Wiedel Photolibrary 100c, 102r, Jeff Morgan 13 14, Lordprice Collection 44, Mary Evans Picture Library 8 (Florence Nightingale), 35, 47, 100t, 101l, Peter Scholey 113b, Picture Partners 81t, Robert Estall Photo Agency 11, Syner-Comm 93, The London Art Archive 36 (Physician), 62, The Print Collector 52, Trinity Mirror / Mirrorpix 92; **Bridgeman Art Library Ltd:** Bibliotheque Nationale Paris, France / Archives Charmet 9 (Medieval doctor), British Library, London, UK / © British Library Board. All Rights Reserved 8 (Leper), 22, 25, 27, 30, Musee de l'Assistance Publique, Hopitaux de Paris, france / Archives Charmet 26, Private Collection 43, 106t, Private Collection / The Stapleton Collection 126, The Royal College of Surgeons, London 109; **British Library Images Online:** The British Library Board; Sloane 2435, f.11v 36 (Barber); **(c) National Portrait Gallery, London:** Purchased with help from the National Lottery through the Heritage Lottery Fund, and Gallery supporters, 2008 9 (Mary Seacole); **City of London:** London Metropolitan Archives 66b; **Corbis:** Aristede Economopoulos / Star Ledger 133l, Bettmann 9 (Plague doctor), 36 (Hospital), 94bl, 115, 118-119, 121cl, Heckmann / dpa 90, Hulton-Deutsch Collection 122bl, The Art Archive 36 (PIlgrims); **Getty Images:** E+ / Jesse Karjalainen 107b, Hulton Archive 66t, 86, SSPL / Science & Society Picture Library 144; **Great Ormond Street Hospital:** NHS Trust 68, 69; **Imperial War Museum:** 74, 130br; **iStockphoto:** Alex Slobodkin 148 (Boxes), Chris Schmidt 148 (Friends), Efendi Kocakafa 148 (TV), Stockphoto4u 150, ZoneCreative 148 (Fruit); **Library of Congress:** 8 (Roman Baths); **Liverpool Record Office:** E. Chambre Hardman Archive 82b; **Look and Learn:** 42; **Mary Evans Picture Library:** 9 (Blood transfusion), 40, 41bl, 45, 54, 59, 60, 64, 67, 82t, 84, Mary Evans ILN Pictures 56; **National Archives:** © Crown Copyright 88; **NHS:** 80; **Press Association Images:** Andy Butterton / PA Archive 89; **Science & Society Picture Library:** Science Museum 8 (Skull); **Science Photo Library Ltd:** A Barrington Brown 94cr, 8 (Hippocrates), 31, 94tr, 94br, 111, 116, 137, 146, Dr. Jeremy Burgess 13, 48r, Mehau Kulyk 9 (DNA), Sheila Terry 9 (Urine chart), 103, 138, Simon Fraser / Royal Victoria Hospital, Newcastle-upon-Tyne 81b, TEK Images 8 (Vaccine), Tom McHugh 8 (Mummy); **Shutterstock.com:** Brasilliao-media 121tl, Jerome Whittingham 19; **The Art Archive:** Biblioteca Nazionale Turin / Giani Dagli Orti 48c; **TopFoto:** Yantman Archives / The Image Works 36 (Apothecary); **Wellcome Library, London:** 9 (Book plate), 21, 38, 41tr, 58, 61, 63, 106b, 107t, 108, 110, 113t, 117, 119tr, 121tr, 125, 130bl, 133tr, 146

Cover images: *Front:* **Corbis:** Bettmann

All other images © Pearson Education

We are grateful to the following for permission to reproduce copyright material:
Source C on page 95 from The Double Helix: A Personal View, Nature April 26, 1974 766-771 (Crick, Francis), W. W. Norton & Co, Nature Publishing Group; Source B on page 114 from Scientific Revolution in Victorian Medicine, Croom Helm (AJ Youngson 19 April 1979); Source D on page 123 from an article by Lister in The British Medical Journal in February 1880, in which Lister responds to criticism of his methods by a surgeon called Mr Spence., The British Medical Journal , February 1880 http://www.bmj.com/content/1/998/237 Source B on page 129 from Joseph Lister and the Story of Antiseptics (Uncharted, Unexplored, and Unexplained: Scientific Advancements of the 19th Century) ISBN-13: 978-1584152620, 12 Nov 2004, Mitchell Lane Publishers (Bankston, John); Source B on page 138 from Article title: CHLOROFORM IN CHOLERA; VOMITING. Author(s): Yeoman Heath, George DOI: 10.1016/S0140-6736(02)58081-8 Date: Oct 1, 1853 Volume: 62 Issue: 1572, Cengage.

Every effort has been made to contact copyright holders of material reproduced in this book. Any omissions will be rectified in subsequent printings if notice is given to the publishers.

Contents

■ Option 1A: Medicine and public health in Britain c50AD to the present day

■ Medicine and public health in Britain c50AD–c1350

■ Medicine and public health c1350–c1750

■ Medicine and public health c1750–c1900

Welcome to this Edexcel GCSE History B: Schools History Project Resource

Option 1A: Medicine and public health in Britain c50AD to the present day and 3A: The transformation of surgery c1845–c1918

These resources are appropriate for GCSE History students on the linear GCSE course certificated from 2015. This course has a focus on change and development through studies of societies in depth and of key themes over time. Packed with exam tips and activities, the book includes lots of engaging features to enthuse students and provide the range of support needed to make teaching and learning a success for all ability levels.

Features of this book

> **Learning outcomes** structure learning at the start of each topic.

> **FASCINATING FACTS** give learning extra depth.

> **Key words** are highlighted and defined for easy reference.

> A topic **Summary** captures the main learning points.

> **◄ Before...** and **After... ►**

These give information about what has happened before and after the period studied to help you piece everything together.

> **Activities** provide stimulating tasks for the classroom and homework.

How to use this book

Edexcel GCSE History B: Schools History Project Medicine and Surgery is divided into the two units in the specification.

Unit 1 is divided into four sections:

- c50AD–c1350
- c1350–c1750
- c1750–c1900
- c1900 to the present day.

At the end of each section there are two spreads, one considering change and continuity and one considering issues concerning source materials.

Unit 3 contains guidance, instruction and practice questions on the source requirements for the exam.

This book does not cover the content for your Unit 2 depth study.

 A dedicated suite of revision resources. We've broken down the six stages of revision to help you ensure that you are prepared every step of the way.

Zone In! How to get into the perfect 'zone' for your revision.

Planning Zone Tips and advice on how to plan your revision effectively.

Know Zone A checklist of things you should know, revision activities and practice exam questions at the end of each unit.

Last-minute advice for just before the exam.

 **Don't Panic Zone** An overview of what you will have to do in the exam, plus a chance to see what a real exam paper will look like.

 Exam Zone What do you do after your exam? This section contains information on how to get your results and answers to frequently asked questions on what to do next.

Zone Out

These features help you to understand how to improve, with guidance on answering exam-style questions, tips on how to remember important concepts and how to avoid common pitfalls.

There are three different types of ExamZone features throughout this book:

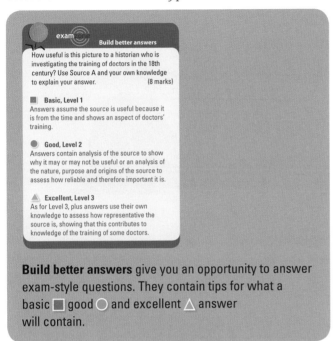

Build better answers give you an opportunity to answer exam-style questions. They contain tips for what a basic ☐ good ○ and excellent △ answer will contain.

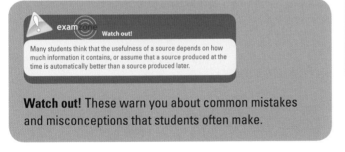

Watch out! These warn you about common mistakes and misconceptions that students often make.

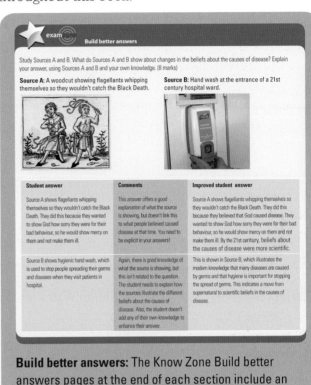

Build better answers: The Know Zone Build better answers pages at the end of each section include an exam-style question with a student answer, comments and an improved answer so that you can see how to improve your own writing.

Medicine and public health

Introduction

This unit will look at developments in medicine from Roman Britain up to the present day. It is separated into the following sections:

- c50AD–c1350
- c1350–c1750
- c1750–c1900
- c1900 to the present day.

You will be asked to think about what changed, why and why at that particular time; whether the change was an improvement; what didn't change and why it didn't.

The pictures on the right show you some of the topics you will study. The leper is an example of someone suffering from an infectious disease in the Middle Ages – nothing could be done to cure leprosy at the time. The second picture shows how science has given us ways to prevent disease and improve people's health – it is a picture of a vaccine for meningitis C.

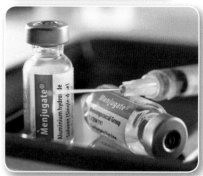

| Before 3000 BC: Prehistoric | 3000 BC to 500 BC: Ancient Egypt | 1000 BC to 250 BC: Ancient Greece | 300 BC to 600 AD: Ancient Rome |

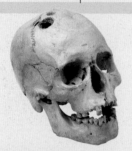

Prehistoric
There is no written evidence, but we have pictures and skeletons that give us some clues about health and medicine.

Ancient Egypt
We have some written evidence and more paintings and artefacts that give us more clues about health and medicine (such as mummies and lists of herbal remedies).

Ancient Greece
By this time we have a wider range of evidence, including pictures, remains of temple buildings and written records from doctors.

Ancient Rome
Here we have even more evidence, such as medical texts, pictures and buildings such as public baths and aqueducts.

Key themes as you work through each period will be:

- What did people think caused illness?
- How did they try to treat and prevent illness?
- Who cared for the sick (including public health)?
- Was there any progress in medicine?
- What factors affected the developments in medicine?

Activity

1 Look at these pictures of doctors (labelled A to D) and put them in chronological order – that means from the earliest in time to the latest.

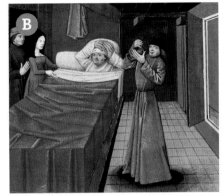

B *A doctor inspecting a patient's urine.*

D *A plague doctor, wearing a mask.*

A *A female doctor examining a pregnant woman.*

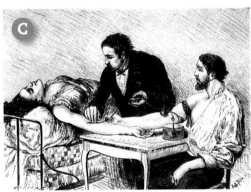

C *An attempted blood transfusion.*

400 to 1500: Middle Ages	1500 to 1750: The Medical Renaissance	1750 to 1900: The Industrial revolution	1900 to present: The modern period

Middle Ages
For this period we can look at evidence from medical texts (both handwritten manuscripts and the earliest printed materials) and buildings such as hospitals.

The Medical Renaissance
This was a period when printed texts became more widely available, so we have a much wider range of evidence.

The industrial revolution
For this period we have a wide range of evidence, such as public records, photographs and medical instruments.

The modern period
For this period, as well as a wide range of written evidence, buildings and instruments, we can also use oral accounts and film.

Answer to Activity 1: the correct order is B, D, C, A.

1.1 Medicine and public health in Britain c50–c1350: introduction

10

This section focuses on medicine and public health in Roman, Anglo-Saxon and **medieval** England to c1350. As you study this, you should focus on the key themes about the process of change in medicine and public health. Those key themes are:

- ideas about the cause and treatment of disease and illness
- approaches to public health and prevention of disease and illness
- the influence of changes in society on medicine and public health.

Before...

- The Ancient Greeks had developed an explanation for ill health based on the idea that it was caused by an imbalance in a person's Four Humours (see page 12). Treatment could be based on changes in diet, and on encouraging the patient to get both rest and exercise. However, treatment could also be based on the idea of letting out excess humour through bleeding or purging the patient.
- At the same time, many people continued to rely on prayers and charms to protect and cure them, or would use home-made remedies based on the use of plants.

After...

- In 1347 the Black Death arrived in Europe and approximately one third of the population died.
- The understanding of disease was very limited and treatment continued to be based on the ideas of Greek doctor Galen (see page 13) but there were discoveries in the 16th and 17th centuries that began to improve the understanding of the body.

Bloodletting: The drawing of blood from a patient by a doctor

Dissection: Cutting open a body to examine its internal structure

Four Humours: A theory that developed in Ancient Greece to explain illness due to an imbalance of blood, phlegm, yellow and black bile in the body

Latrine: Something used as a communal toilet (individual latrines were called privies)

Medieval: A name for the 'Middle Ages', the period between the Ancient World (which ended when the Romans left Britain) and the Renaissance of the 16th and 17th centuries

Physician: A trained doctor

Public health: The standard of living conditions and general health of the people

Purging: Getting rid of bad or excess Humours by making someone sick or by making them have diarrhoea

Society: The way a group of people links together in some common ways

Supernatural: Forces outside nature that some people believe can affect events, for example, God, charms and luck, witchcraft or astrology

Surgeon: Someone who deals with wounds or with treatment that involves cutting the body

> **FASCINATING FACT**
> Archeologists have discovered that Roman Britons used toilet sponges instead of paper and disinfected them in vinegar.

460 BC – c375 BC
Hippocrates

43 AD
Britain became part of the Roman Empire

129 – 216
Galen

410
Romans left Britain

597
Ethelbert, ruler of Kent, was converted to Christianity by St Augustine

664
Control of Pope in Rome extended over Christian Church in Britain

c930
Leechbook of Bald

1348
Black Death reached Britain

1.2 What were your chances of survival in Roman Britain?

Learning outcome

By the end of this topic you should be able to:

- give reasons why life expectancy did increase for some people, but not everyone, after the Romans arrived in Britain

Activities

1 List reasons why public health was so important to the Romans.

2 Explain why having good public health provision is related to having a central government.

The good news!

When the Romans conquered Britain in 43AD, they brought their ideas with them. The Roman Empire relied on having healthy citizens to keep it running – healthy soldiers so the army could keep the peace, and healthy workers, traders and farmers to keep the Empire wealthy and fed. This meant that the Romans were interested in what they could do to improve health, though they were less interested in what caused illness in the first place.

The Romans also brought one system of government to the whole of their conquered territory in Britain. Both of these factors led to major improvements in **public health**, meaning more people had access to clean water and sewage systems. People also benefited from the public baths that sprang up in most towns so they could keep clean, fit and healthy.

This meant that many people stood a better chance of living longer than they had before the Romans came because the emphasis on hygiene and fitness meant people stood less chance of getting ill.

Source A: This shows the main bathing area of the Roman baths in Bath today – one of the best preserved Roman remains in the world.

The not so good news

The Romans adopted many of their ideas about disease and illness from the Greeks and there were few developments by the Romans about theories of illness. For the Britons, this brought them some new treatments such as **bloodletting** - if they could afford to see a **physician**. However, for most people, if they became ill or injured they relied on the same herbal remedies and prayed to their old gods to make them well - as they had always done. This meant that, if you did become ill, your chances of recovering were little better than they had been before the Romans arrived.

Moreover, as more people moved into towns, there was more crowding and therefore disease could spread more quickly. Also, as soldiers and merchants moved from country to country and town to town, there was more chance of diseases spreading over further distances.

Summary

The Romans brought many changes to public health in England, which led to some people becoming healthier and therefore living longer. However, there was little progress in medical understanding and treatment, which meant that, if you did become ill, your chances of survival were no greater than before. So life expectancy didn't improve for everyone.

1.3 Medical ideas from the Ancient World

Learning outcomes

By the end of this topic you should be able to:

- understand that many Roman ideas were influenced by Greek ideas
- explain the idea of ill health being the result of an imbalance in the Four Humours
- provide examples of treatments based on the Four Humours
- explain the link between ideas and treatments and provide examples

The influence of Hippocrates on Roman medicine

The Ancient Greek doctor Hippocrates died in about c375BC but he had a huge influence on doctors' training and ideas about the causes of disease in the Roman Empire. Hippocrates did not believe disease was sent by the gods. He believed illness had a physical, rational basis and could therefore be treated. His ideas were written down by his followers and were used by doctors for many centuries.

- Hippocrates said that a doctor should respect all life; if a doctor didn't know how to treat an illness, he should not try anything that could be harmful.

- Hippocrates developed the Theory of the Four Humours as an explanation for illness. Treatment was based on the idea of letting out excess Humours to cure or prevent illness.

- Hippocrates developed the approach that became known as Clinical Observation, saying the doctor should:
  - study the patient's symptoms (breathing, heartbeat, temperature, and urine) and ask about how the illness had developed;
  - make notes and use knowledge of similar cases to predict what was likely to happen next;
  - once the predictions were shown to be accurate, correctly diagnose the illness and treat it – preferably through diet, exercise or rest.

The Four Humours

The Ancient Greeks identified four different liquids, or Humours, in the body:

- blood
- phlegm (the watery liquid when you sneeze or cough)
- yellow bile (when you are sick)
- black bile (we think this was probably blood in your vomit, which makes the liquid look black).

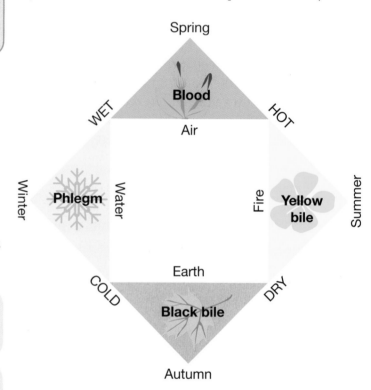

Humour	Season	Element	Qualities	Ancient name
Blood	Spring	Air	Hot & wet	Sanguine
Yellow bile	Summer	Fire	Hot & dry	Choleric
Black bile	Autumn	Earth	Cold & dry	Melancholic
Phlegm	Winter	Water	Cold & wet	Phlegmatic

The Greeks thought that every person had their own individual mix of these Four Humours and that if this mix was unbalanced you became ill (see the diagram). So, if you had a temperature, your skin went red and hot because you had too much blood, whereas a dark lump was the result of too much black bile.

They also thought that these Humours were linked to the four seasons and their idea of four elements (earth, air, fire and water). Therefore, in winter, which is linked to water, they believed that your body produces too much phlegm and you have to sneeze and cough to get rid of it.

This theory helped to explain why people became ill and sometimes treatment tried to restore the balance of the Four Humours, for example, by letting out excess blood. However, Hippocrates suggested that most treatment should be based on rest, changes in diet and leaving the body to heal itself.

The influence of Galen on Roman medicine

Claudius Galen was a Greek doctor who worked in Rome in the 2nd century AD. He developed the Theory of the Four Humours further. He believed very strongly in bloodletting as a treatment for almost all illnesses and also suggested that the balance of a person's Four Humours could be restored by his Theory of Opposites. He suggested that, if you had too much phlegm, which is linked to water and cold, you should eat hot peppers; if you had a temperature, you should eat cucumber, which would cool you down.

Galen had experience as a **surgeon** treating gladiators. He also carried out **dissections**, although these were mainly on animals. His most famous experiment was where he cut certain nerves in a pig's spinal cord to prove that movement and the voice were controlled by the brain.

Source A: The dissection of a pig by Galen.

Galen produced over 350 texts about medicine and surgery, which summarised medical knowledge at the time. He explained his new ideas and linked them with existing theories, making them into one coherent system. He was very confident and boldly claimed that he had now perfected Ancient Greek ideas, and therefore many people believed that there was no point in any further medical research.

Summary

Many ideas in Roman medicine were based on Greek theories, especially the idea of the Four Humours. There were some developments, such as Galen's Theory of Opposites, and his increased knowledge of anatomy and how the body works.

1.4 Roman medicine and treatment

Learning outcomes

By the end of this topic you should be able to:

- understand that Roman explanations for disease included a mix of supernatural and rational explanations
- explain who treated the sick in Roman Britain and where
- give examples of some of the different treatments for disease

Roman ideas about disease

The Romans had several explanations for the causes of disease:

- that there was a **supernatural** reason, for example that disease was sent by the gods or was a curse
- that it was caused by bad air from swamps or places where there were bad smells (they realised that hygiene was linked to health, although they didn't understand why)
- that it was caused by an imbalance of a person's humours.

These ideas had an impact on how people treated disease.

What did people do when they needed treatment?

There were very few doctors in Roman Britain and most illnesses were treated within the home, usually by the father of the family, using remedies passed down from his father. Those who could afford, and had access to, a trained doctor were treated in their own homes too.

There were some hospitals, mainly in forts, and these were reserved for soldiers. They were often well equipped and provided excellent training for both surgeons and physicians, especially in treating wounds and injuries. However, there were few hospitals open to the public, so this treatment and training would have had very little impact on the lives of ordinary people.

Source A: Ruins of a Roman temple in Monmouthshire in Britain. People who were sick often visited the temple for help.

Many people visited a temple to make offerings to gods or consult with priests. People also visited public baths (see page 16) as it was believed the water had healing properties.

Pregnant women relied on other women to help them through child birth. Some women became very experienced at this and were used as midwives by many families in a town or village.

Medical treatments

Remedies in Roman Britain included some made from herbs and plants (such as a saffron salve for sore eyes) but also included ideas such as using oil and newly cut wool to relieve aches and inflammations. Many of these treatments were used throughout the Roman Empire.

Source B: The Roman writer, Pliny, described some of the medical treatments used.

> Unwashed wool supplies very many remedies… it is applied… with honey to old sores. Wounds it heals if dipped in wine or vinegar… yolks of eggs… are taken for dysentery with the ash of their shells, poppy juice and wine. It is recommended to bathe the eyes with a decoction of the liver and to apply the marrow to those that are painful or swollen.

In the 2nd century, the Roman writer Dioscorides published a book with detailed information on the use of plants and herbs as drugs.

FASCINATING FACT
Some people thought cabbage was so good for health that they recommended using the urine of someone who had lived on a cabbage diet to wash children to make their muscles strong.

Some of the medical ideas of the Celts already living in Britain were replaced by Roman ideas, but others were incorporated into Roman medicine; for example, the religious group called Druids made great use of British herbs and plants, and the Romans continued this. The Romans also believed that diet, exercise and rest were very important in treating illness as well as preventing it. Other treatments might consist of bloodletting or **purging**, but often the Romans would mix these practical remedies with prayers and offerings made to Salus, the god of health.

Activities

1 Draw a memory map of all the different people you might get medical help from in Roman Britain.

2 Explain why treatment for illness was often a mixture of practical aspects, such as herbal remedies or bloodletting, and superstitious aspects, such as carrying charms or making offerings to the gods.

3 Make a list of possible medical treatments in Roman Britain. Which of these were 'new' and which of them would have existed before the Romans arrived?

exam zone

Build better answers

Choose one period and describe the key ideas about the causes of disease in England during that period:
• Roman Britain
• The later Middle Ages.   (6 marks)

■ **Basic, Level 1**
Answers offer one or two ideas which are not described in detail, such as *'everyone thought disease was brought by the gods'.*

● **Good, Level 2**
Answers include a range of ideas and detail for each, such as describing different supernatural reasons for disease and more rational ideas such as the theory of the Four Humours or bad air/smells.

Summary

There were various supernatural as well as rational ideas about the causes of disease in Roman Britain. Treatments were also a mix of the practical and superstitious. A variety of people treated the sick, but very few people used trained doctors as there were very few of them and they were expensive.

1.5 Public health in Roman Britain

Learning outcomes

By the end of this topic you should be able to:

- understand the key features of Roman public health
- explain the links between features of Roman society and public health

The Romans noticed that disease seemed to increase if you lived near marshes and swamps. This led them to build in healthy places, away from swamps, because bad air (which they called miasma) caused disease. They also recognised that there was a link between dirt and disease and, although they could not explain what the link was, they stressed the need to provide access to clean water, to remove sewage and for people to keep themselves clean.

Public baths

Most Roman towns in Britain had public baths (remains have been found at Caerleon in Wales, Canterbury, Exeter and Leicester). Admission was not free but it was cheap enough for most people to attend and many visited every day. The baths served a variety of functions:

- **Social** They were a place for people to meet, both for pleasure and to discuss business.
- **Hygiene** They provided the means for people to keep clean.
- **Exercise** They provided places where people could keep fit. The Romans were big fans of being fit and strong!
- **Medical** They believed the waters had healing powers, so people with illnesses or ailments regularly visited the baths as they believed it would make them better.

The actual baths were just one part of a whole complex of facilities.

1 Before going into the baths both men and women would have done some exercise in the exercise hall: activities such as wrestling or ball games for men, games or weights for women.

2 Public toilets in the baths were much less private than we are used to, but waste was removed from the baths by a sewage system and users had fresh water to clean their hands with. They would also rinse the sponge they had used to wipe their bottoms.

3 Bathers next went into a series of warm rooms; these could be steamy and damp like a Turkish bath, or a dry heat like a sauna. Here people were massaged with oil and then the oil was scraped off with a scraper called a strigil. This was a very effective way of removing dirt from the body.

4 After steaming themselves in warm and hot water or saunas, Roman bathers would finish with a dip in a cold pool: the frigidarium. They would have left the baths a lot cleaner and more relaxed than when they arrived!

Water and waste

The Romans built complex water systems to bring fresh water into towns and even some people's homes.

Fresh water from springs in the hills was transported to towns via pipes and aqueducts.

↓

Water was stored in reservoirs near the towns.

↓

Pipes carried the water from reservoirs into the towns, to public wells or fountains, public baths and toilets and the private houses of the rich.

Sanitation was also important to the Romans and they built sewage systems which took waste away from public baths, toilets and houses and emptied into rivers away from the town. The remains of underground sewerage systems have been found at York, Lincoln and Colchester.

The Roman system of piped water and sewers was impressive and far better than anything Britain had had before. It enabled many people to stay healthy and did prevent some disease. However, most towns and cities had open drains. Also, when the water supply was low there wasn't enough for the sewers to work properly, so waste built up and made disease more likely.

Roman society

There were three main factors that made public health important to the Romans as well as enabling them to put the systems in place.

1 Government
- Made central decisions.
- Organised large-scale projects.
- Raised taxes to pay for projects and provided the manpower to carry them out.

2 Army
- Needed good standard of public health.
- Contained soldiers from all over the empire who brought ideas as well as manpower.
- During peacetime, they built roads, baths, sewers, etc.

3 Communications
- Good quality roads made travel and therefore communication easier and quicker across the Empire.
- Central control from Rome and regular changes of officials kept Britain up-to-date with new ideas.
- Knowledge and ideas (for example of plants and herbs) spread as people travelled throughout the Empire.

Activities

1 Design a brochure to explain the benefits of fresh water, sewers and public baths to the uncivilised people of Roman Britain. (Be careful to include only knowledge available at the time, so do not include references to germs, for example.)

2 Explain the interaction between the army, the government and improvement in communications as factors that made the Roman public health system possible in Britain. Which factor do you think was most important?

3 'The main contribution the Romans made to medical progress was in public health rather than in the understanding and treatment of disease.' How far do you agree with this statement?

Summary

Public health was a major feature of Roman civilisation and many towns in Britain benefited from having public baths, a clean water supply and an organised system of sanitation.

1.6 What changed when the Romans left?

18

Learning outcomes

By the end of this topic you should be able to:

- outline and explain what happened to public health systems when the Romans left Britain
- understand the increasing importance of Christianity to medicine and treatment

The period from after the Roman army left in 410AD, to around 1000AD, saw some huge changes in **society** that had an impact on medicine and public health.

The collapse of the Roman Empire had a huge impact on parts of Britain. Instead of being one country ruled by Rome, Roman Britain fractured into smaller kingdoms which often fought with each other. Each kingdom was ruled by a different king.

Loss of the Roman army

- No-one to maintain law and order amongst the locals.
- No engineering or builders to keep the public health systems in towns running.
- No-one to stop invasions – in the 5th and 6th centuries, Britain was invaded by illiterate tribes from Europe – the Angles, Saxons and Jutes.

What happened after the Romans left?

Loss of one ruler or government

- No overall control to commission or pay for public health schemes to be built or maintained.
- The priority for the new rulers was trying to keep and expand their kingdoms – they couldn't afford the time or money for public health systems or education.

Wars and chaos

- Led to the destruction of libraries and books as well as to towns themselves.
- It became far more dangerous to travel, so ideas and people became stuck in their local settlements.
- As people's possessions, crops and livelihoods were destroyed by conflict, poverty increased.

exam zone — Build better answers

To what extent did medical progress stop when the Romans withdrew from England? Explain your answer. You may use the following in your answer:

- Public health
- Medical training

You must also include information of your own.

(16 marks)

▪ **Basic, Level 1** Answer makes simple statements about what happened when the Romans left.

● **Good, Level 2** Answer provides detailed description of Roman or medieval medicine and states there was some decline or continuity.

▲ **Better, Level 3** Answer shows some comparison of medicine in Roman Britain and in the Middle Ages.

▲ **Excellent, Level 4** Answer shows detailed comparison of both continuity and change in medicine in Roman Britain and in the Middle Ages, supported by accurate material from both the stimulus, and from own knowledge e.g. the influence of the Church.

Make sure you write accurately – there are three extra marks available for spelling, grammar and punctuation in these questions.

Impact on medicine and public health

Perhaps the most profound impact of the collapse of the Roman Empire was on public health systems, which gradually stopped working or were destroyed by war. Although many towns were abandoned, as people went back to living as farmers in villages, when towns started to grow again it meant they were far more unhygienic. Disease therefore became more of a problem.

The other impact of the Roman withdrawal on medicine was that trained physicians almost totally disappeared, because:

- Books and libraries where medical knowledge had been kept were destroyed.
- The new rulers were illiterate and not interested in educating doctors anyway.
- People no longer travelled very far so couldn't travel to obtain learning and training.
- The huge increase in poverty meant that nobody could afford a trained physician.

Increasing importance of Christianity

After the Romans left, and especially after the Norman invasion in 1066, Christianity became increasingly important in society and therefore in medicine and treatment.

- It was an international organisation across all Europe – an important channel of communication.
- Most priests could read and write and senior churchmen were often included among the king's advisers.
- Learning was preserved in the libraries of monasteries and convents.
- Monasteries and convents often had an infirmarian, who cared for the sick.
- People believed very strongly in religion and accepted the Church's authority over their lives.
- People believed illness was a sign of sin, a punishment, or a test sent by God.

Source A: A photograph of York Minster.

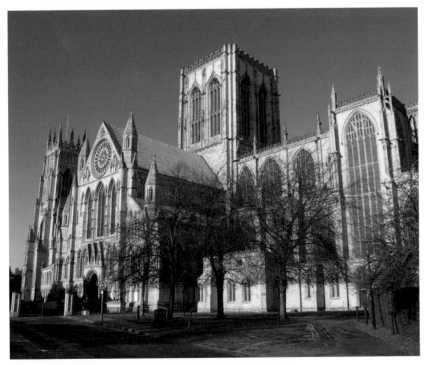

Activities

1   How might the collapse of public health systems have affected people's health? Create a flow chart or diagram which shows the impact of the collapse on public health in Britain.

2   In what ways did the increasing importance of the Christian Church affect medicine?

Summary

The decline of public health systems and the growth of the importance of Christianity are two of the biggest changes in medicine from 50 to 1350.

1.7 Medicine and treatment in the Middle Ages in Britain

Learning outcomes

By the end of this topic you should be able to:

- understand the medical treatments used in the Middle Ages
- understand the reasons why there was so little progress in medicine during the Middle Ages
- evaluate the nature and extent of progress in medical treatment during the Middle Ages

The labels 'Middle Ages' and 'medieval' are used by historians to describe the period between the Ancient World and the modern period, although they are not very exact (they are also not so relevant when studying Islamic, African, American or Asian history).

Treatment in the Middle Ages – no big change?

The Romans left Britain in 410. With no one taking responsibility for maintaining the structures built by the Romans, the public health facilities in towns fell into ruins. Although this had some effect on health and hygiene, it did not affect ideas about disease, and so the withdrawal of the Romans had limited impact on the treatments being used in medicine. Apart from Galen's Theory of Opposites, the Romans had shown little interest in developing their understanding of disease and illness any further. They had taken a practical attitude, which had included using local herbs and praying to local gods, and this meant that there was not a big change in medicine when the Romans left Britain.

People in the Middle Ages worked out many of the cures they used through a process of trial and error. They remembered successful remedies and repeated them even though they did not understand why they worked.

Honey was a common ingredient – but not just to make the medicine taste nice; it seemed to help sore throats and cuts. We now know that honey has antibiotic properties and therefore using it as a drink or an ointment would have helped to prevent infection.

FASCINATING FACT

A cure for toothache was to mix equal amounts of ground acorn, henbane seeds and wax and form the mixture into a candle. The smoke was to be directed into the mouth and a black cloth held underneath the mouth. It was thought the worm that was causing the toothache would fall onto the cloth.

Onions, garlic, wine and lichen from trees were also used often and all have some antibiotic properties.

Most folk remedies were passed down by word of mouth, but knowledge of plants and healing was sometimes written down in leechbooks (leech means healer). The most famous one is known as the Leechbook of Bald (Bald was the person who owned the book). A book of remedies written in the 13th century by Rhiwallon of Myddfai in Wales, it was unusual because it gave specific quantities of ingredients and methods of preparation whereas most recipes just named the plants involved.

Religion and superstition

As you have seen, the Christian Church became increasingly important during the Middle Ages. This had a huge impact on many aspects of medicine - including treatment. People would say prayers and make offerings and might also go on a pilgrimage to a holy shrine in the hope that God would cure them. However, many people would also carry a lucky charm or carry out a superstitious ritual such as rubbing snail juice on their eyes to cure blindness.

As learning increased during the 12th century, there was a great deal of interest in the stars and in astrology. Scholars linked these star signs to the Greek idea of the four elements: earth, air, fire and water. These astrological ideas were then linked to Galen's ideas on medicine. For example, doctors believed that an operation on the head should be avoided when the moon is in the sign of Aries.

Physicians often used handbooks, called 'vade mecum', which is Latin for 'Go with me'. These manuals would include urine charts, where the physician could compare the colour of the patient's urine to help him diagnose the illness, or a zodiac chart (see source A) to help the physician to know when to avoid certain treatments. There were also books such as the Compendium of Medicine, written by Gilbertus Anglicus (Gilbert the Englishman). This was in Latin because it was intended for educated physicians and it helped the physician to diagnose and treat a range of illnesses. Herbals, which described plants and their uses in medicine, were in English because they were used by ordinary people in folk remedies.

The influence of Galen

In the towns, richer people might consult a physician who was likely to use treatments that were based on the Four Humours and the Theory of Opposites. Galen's ideas continued to be the basis of medical training for doctors.

Galen had been particularly keen on using bloodletting, both as a healing method and as a way to prevent illness. This was usually done by opening a vein and letting blood drip out into a bleeding bowl (these often had measuring lines around the inside to check how much blood had been lost) or by attaching leeches to the body (leeches suck blood and then detach themselves when they are full).

However, physicians also prescribed medicines based on a wide range of ingredients, such as plants, herbs and spices, and also ground minerals or the bezoar (a stone found in the stomach of goats in Persia).

Source A: A medieval diagram showing which zodiac signs and times of the year were linked to the different parts of the body.

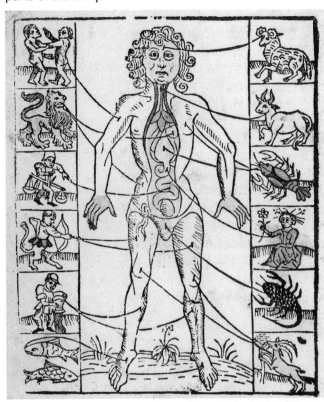

Activities

1. What examples can you find of medical ideas and treatment continuing from the Roman period into the Middle Ages?
2. What examples can you find of new aspects of medicine in the Middle Ages?
3. What factors affected the development of medicine from the Roman period to the Middle Ages?
4. Why was there such an emphasis on religion, superstition and tradition in medieval Britain?
5. How far does the evidence suggest that medicine did not progress in the Middle Ages?

Summary

In the early Middle Ages there seemed to be little change in the sort of treatments being used for illness. The trained physician usually followed Galen's ideas, but there was little understanding of disease and therefore these treatments had little effect. Patients often combined treatment with prayers and charms.

1.8 Public health in the Middle Ages

Learning outcomes

By the end of this topic you should be able to:

- understand the public health problems in the Middle Ages
- understand the role of government in public health provision during the Middle Ages
- understand the extent of progress or regress in public health during the Middle Ages

As towns grew bigger throughout the Middle Ages, the problems of hygiene became more important. People recognised there was a link between dirt and disease, even though they could not explain what that link was, but it was difficult to keep towns clean.

The biggest public health problems in towns were caused by:

- Lack of clean water – **latrines** (toilets) were often built directly over rivers where people got water from.
- No means of removing sewage – it remained in open drains, cesspits or was flushed into rivers or streams.
- The remains of butchered animals were often left on the streets, which attracted rats and mice.

Why was London so smelly?

London, as the largest city in Britain, had the biggest problems. In the 13th century, lead pipes (paid for by the city authorities and from money given by individuals) were laid to provide water from the River Tyburn. However, there were leaks, the water was often contaminated and the supply was not enough for the city. Even when water was bought from a water seller, there was no guarantee that it would be clean. In fact, the quality of water was so poor that very few people actually drank it and most drank ale instead.

Meanwhile, animal and human excrement was common in the streets, rubbish was not removed, butchers slaughtered animals and left the remains in the street and rats were common. Laws were regularly passed, especially in times of disease, but they only had a limited effect – the systems were just too undeveloped to deal with the problem.

There were public latrines in London (and in places such as Leicester, Winchester, Hull, Scarborough, Southampton and Exeter) but we also know that people sometimes just relieved themselves in the street – in fact, one beggar boy died when he was run over by a carriage as he squatted in the street.

Source A: A picture of an English water seller drawn in 1338.

FASCINATING FACTS

In London in the 14th century it took approximately 100 barrels to remove the contents of a privy that was used by several households.

All this suggests that during the Middle Ages there was no progress in public health and that the standard of public health had regressed (gone backwards), especially in the towns and cities.

However, there were some attempts to improve hygiene.

1281 The government attempted to stop pigs being allowed in London's streets.

Government attempts to improve hygiene in towns and cities.

1347 Sanitary Act tried to keep the streets cleaner.

1388 a parliamentary statute complained that 'dung and filth... in ditches, rivers and other waters... so that the air there is grown greatly corrupt and infected and many intolerable diseases happen'.

On the other hand…

The situation was not completely bad. Rich people often had good standards of hygiene and would bathe in a wooden tub; many had a privy (a private latrine) built so that human waste was kept away from the living areas. Archaeologists have found that many houses belonging to merchants and bishops had lead pipes for a water supply, latrines and stone sewers.

Monks and nuns lived simple lives but the standard of hygiene in monasteries and convents was usually high. There would be fresh water piped to the building and the latrines were usually built over running water, which would take away the human waste.

Town councils recognised the importance of public health. Southampton improved its water supply in the 15th century after a merchant left a bequest for that purpose and, despite the problems of leaky pipes and contamination, London, Exeter and Bristol did have supplies of fresh water running through pipes or conduits to the cities. There were also large baths, known as stewes, where people bathed together in large wooden tubs. Among the rich, this could be a very social occasion, with food and drink being shared, but the public stewes in towns were often denounced by the Church for leading to immoral behaviour.

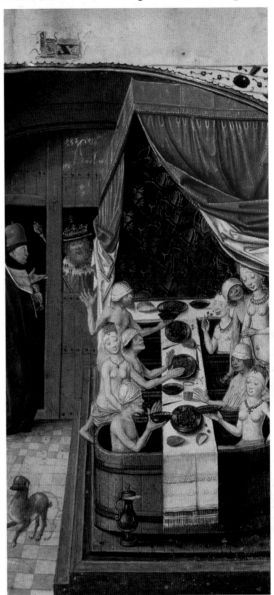

Source B: Public bathing in the Middle Ages.

Activities

1 Make a list of all the public health issues connected with living in a town.

2 Town councils passed laws fairly regularly about keeping the streets clean, often repeating the same law a few years later. What does this suggest about the role of the local authorities in maintaining a good standard of public health?

3 Why do you think so few regulations were passed to improve public health in the countryside and villages?

4 Find examples of public health between the Roman period and the Middle Ages to show progress (improvements), stagnation (things staying the same) and regress (things getting worse).

Challenge

5 Research your nearest large town or city that has a Roman past. What public health did that city have in Roman times? What evidence is there of the local authorities trying to improve public health in the Middle Ages?

Summary

In Roman times, central and local government had a duty to provide a good standard of public health for the towns and used taxes and the army to do this. The situation in the Middle Ages was different and there was little organised provision of water or sanitation. The rich were not affected by this because they could pay for a better standard of living, and peasants were not too badly affected because the villages were not crowded. It was the poor people in towns who were the most badly affected.

1.9 Medical training from Roman Britain to c1350

24

Learning outcomes

By the end of this topic you should be able to:

- understand how medical training changed during the period from Roman Britain to c1350
- understand the factors affecting changes in medical training during this period
- evaluate the progress in medical training during this period

In the Roman period doctors were not highly respected. It could be seen that many of their treatments did not work and because many of the doctors in Rome were Greeks, the Romans felt that the foreign doctors were trying to take advantage of them. When Galen publicised his methods, many doctors hated him because he was arrogant and criticized their old methods – as well as being a foreigner!

- Alexandria in Egypt was the main centre of medical training because doctors there were allowed to dissect human bodies.
- The library at Alexandria held works from Greece, Egypt and India.
- There was no requirement for doctors to be formally trained.
- Most doctors 'trained' by reading books such as the Hippocratic Collection (the ideas of Hippocrates, collected and written down by his followers), or by working with someone who was already a successful doctor.
- There was no organization to check that doctors were knowledgeable or to follow up complaints about bad doctors.
- Anyone who wanted to be a doctor could just set up in business.

At this time, medicine was thought to be closely linked to philosophy, and medical treatment was therefore part of a more holistic analysis of the person and their lifestyle. This explains why the idea of the Four Humours was so widely accepted and why treatment was often based on diet, exercise and changes to the patient's lifestyle, such as taking baths or getting more sleep. However, Roman medical ideas also gradually began to incorporate knowledge of plants and treatments from different countries throughout the Empire.

The effect of Roman medicine on Britain was fairly limited because Britain was on the edge of the Roman Empire and therefore few doctors would make the journey to Britain. However, each of the army legions sent there brought their own surgeons and, as some Romans settled there, their medical ideas began to spread. Although the Druid priests already in Britain had a good knowledge of plants and herbal remedies, this knowledge was passed on from person to person and was not written down. This meant that, by the time the Romans left Britain, most doctors were following Roman medical ideas.

For the few centuries after the Romans left, trained physicians almost totally disappeared from England (see pages 18–19). However, Christian monasteries and convents had libraries that preserved many books. As society became more stable, some of these became centres of learning. Some grew into universities and offered training in the 'Arts', which included the study of rhetoric, geometry, astronomy and music. At first, medical training was undertaken in addition to a study of the Arts and took a total of ten years, so there were few doctors who trained in this way.

FASCINATING FACT

Books were so precious in the Middle Ages that they were often chained to library shelves.

Source A: A 14th-century picture showing a physician treating a patient; the people behind the physician may be his apprentices.

juli eltoit li kois trouble; a
iour en iour et bruoit tantd

However, by the 12th century a separate course had developed and medical training was based on a set of texts that became known as the Ars Medicinae (Art of Medicine), including some works written by Muslim scholars. By the 13th century, most towns would not let a doctor set up a medical practice unless he could prove he had completed several years of study.

Education and training were controlled by the Church, and ideas and treatment were therefore slow to change. In particular, the Church approved of Galen and his ideas. He had lived before Christianity became a major religion, but he believed in a soul and he said that the parts of the body had been created to work together. These ideas fitted in well with Church beliefs). Medical teaching was based on reinforcing Galen's ideas, and students were not encouraged to study anatomy or look for mistakes in his teachings.

The medical schools gradually became independent from the Church so that, by the time of the Reformation in the 16th century, the Church had lost control of medical training.

Activities

1 Why were there so few doctors in Roman Britain?

2 Why would many people in the Middle Ages have little confidence in a doctor?

3 Write a letter from a doctor who has just qualified to the head of a noble family in your area asking to be appointed to the household. Explain why you would be a good doctor.

4 Why was it significant that medical training eventually became independent from the Church?

Summary

The standard of knowledge and training of physicians did not change much between the Roman period and the early Middle Ages, apart from a blip for a few centuries after the Romans left. In the 12th century life became more settled in Europe. As trade increased and the economy improved, towns grew much larger and learning increased. Universities and medical schools began to be set up and there was a greater emphasis on training for physicians. However, the level of knowledge and the sort of treatments used still did not change very much.

1.10 Hospitals

Learning outcomes

By the end of this topic you should be able to:

- understand the types of hospitals that were established during the Middle Ages
- understand the role played by the Church and hospitals in medical treatment
- evaluate the significance of the role played by hospitals in medical treatment

As you saw on page 14, Roman hospitals were for the army; it was expected that other people who were sick would be cared for by their families. In the Middle Ages, hospitals were originally guest houses, and were usually part of a monastery or convent, offering hospitality to travellers. The first hospital in the sense that we use the term, of caring for the sick, was the Hotel Dieu, set up in Paris in the 7th century.

Care not cure

Over 1,000 hospitals were established in England and Wales during the Middle Ages. Many of them were founded through charitable donations, for example St Bartholomew's in London in 1123. They were usually quite small (often they had 12 inmates in memory of Jesus' 12 disciples), although there were some large-scale hospitals, for example St Leonard's in York could admit over 200 patients.

These hospitals were usually run by monks and nuns as part of their Christian duties because Jesus had said his followers should care for the sick. The Benedictine monks made this a major part of their rules. There was also thought to be a strong link between religion and ill health because illness was often seen as a punishment for your sins. In addition, your outward body was often thought to reflect your character and soul, and therefore any disfigurement was interpreted as a sign of sin and evil. Therefore, the monks and nuns aimed to care for the sick but not to cure them. Consequently, no doctor was appointed to St Bartholomew's, but several priests were, as it was felt that patients needed spiritual support more than medical treatment.

In fact, people with infectious diseases or incurable conditions often would not be admitted.

This approach may seem strange to us but it is similar to the holistic approach used in many alternative medicines. Care for the soul, combined with the rest, warmth, food and care that patients received, could have meant that some patients did actually get better.

Source A: A picture of a convent in France showing the typical layout of a hospital. Notice that the patients are sharing beds, although the covers and pillows are clean.

The food given to the patients at St Anthony's hospital, in London, included fresh salmon, turbot, shrimps, plaice, pork, capons, beef, geese, veal, rabbit, damsons, pears and apples. Although this was a wealthy hospital and the food was not typical, many hospitals grew a wide range of fresh fruit and vegetables.

The beds would also be positioned so that the patients could see the altar, religious statues and images in stained glass windows to help them focus on religion and be healed.

examzone
Build better answers

What do Sources A and B show about the uses of hospitals in the Middle Ages? Explain your answer, using Sources A and B and your own knowledge.

(8 marks)

 Basic, Level 1
Answer gives a basic comment, without providing support from the sources or from own knowledge.

 Good, Level 2
Answer gives a more detailed comment on the sources and/or from their own knowledge.

△ **Excellent, Level 3**
Answer comments in detail on what the sources show using both the sources themselves and own knowledge.

Source B: A drawing of a leper in the medieval period. He is carrying a bell to warn people to keep away.

Activities

1 Explain why many medieval hospitals were run by monks and nuns rather than physicians.

2 Why were the walls of most hospitals decorated with Christian religious scenes, especially the Last Judgement?

3 Draw a storyboard about a leper who is turned away from an almshouse and a hospital and is sent to the leper house. Include speech bubbles to explain why he is turned away until he gets to the leper house.

4 What does the treatment of lepers show about approaches to infectious diseases in the Middle Ages?

In the Great Hospital at Norwich, founded in 1249 by Bishop Walter de Suffield, women were welcome as nurses, but Bishop Suffield did not allow female patients and any women employed within the hospital had to be aged 50 or over, so that they would not distract the patients from their prayers.

Almshouses

Almshouses began to be set up in the 14th century to care for the 'deserving' poor and old. These people were expected to live according to quite strict rules about behaviour and prayer. Although they were cared for when they were unwell, the almshouse was not intended to be a hospital providing medical treatment.

Case study: the treatment of leprosy

Leper houses or lazars were places for lepers to live. Leprosy is a very unpleasant disease in which the nerve endings die and body extremities, such as fingers and toes, can decay and leave sufferers deformed. In the Middle Ages it was incurable. Throughout Europe lepers were expected to keep themselves apart from other people because they were infectious (they even had to carry a bell and ring it to warn people to move away).

No treatment was available so the leper houses only aimed to provide care for the sufferers. Many were set up in the 12th and 13th centuries when there was an epidemic of leprosy but similar 'pest houses' were built later to isolate sufferers from the plague, which was also called the Great Mortality or the pestilence.

Summary

Religion was closely linked to medicine in the Middle Ages. Many hospitals were run by monks and nuns and provided care for the sick but they did not aim to provide medical treatment.

1.11 Influence of social change on medicine and public health

28

The role of religion

Emperor Constantine converted to Christianity in 313, making it one of the official religions of the Roman Empire; after that, Christianity quickly became the main religion in Europe. As the Roman Empire collapsed, the Church was left as the only international organisation that could preserve and transmit knowledge.

As you have seen, the role of the Church was an important one in controlling the training of physicians and in preserving the ideas of Galen. Religion also affected people's reactions to the Black Death (see pages 34–35) and to the use of dissections.

Many religious saints came to be associated with specific conditions, so you would pray to St Anthony if you had a skin complaint, St Blaise if you had a sore throat or St James if you had rheumatism. It was also felt that the king, who was anointed with holy oil at his coronation, had religious powers. Scrofula was a form of tuberculosis (TB) that affected glands in the neck, and it was felt that, if the king laid his hands on a sufferer, the disease could be cured – regular ceremonies were held, often around Easter time.

Religious institutions such as monasteries and convents often did a lot of caring work for the sick. The diagram in Source A shows how care for the sick was a central part of life at Fountains Abbey, in Yorkshire.

A painting of Fountains Abbey in Yorkshire.

Source A: A diagram of the floor plan of Fountains Abbey in Yorkshire.

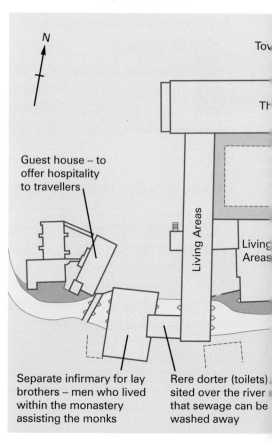

Guest house – to offer hospitality to travellers

Living Areas

Living Areas

Separate infirmary for lay brothers – men who lived within the monastery assisting the monks

Rere dorter (toilets) sited over the river that sewage can be washed away

The role of government

After the end of the Roman Empire, the rulers in Britain were more concerned with protecting their people and trade from attack than with improving medicine. Even after the Norman Conquest in 1066, when the kings began to increase their control over the country, medicine was not a priority. This was partly because the Church controlled so many aspects of medicine and partly because there seemed to be very little that government could actually do.

In the Roman period, the government organized and funded the construction of a good system of public health but, after the Romans, when kings and central government did not make such work a priority, the standard of public health fell and local authorities faced many problems in trying to keep their towns clean.

People understood that cleanliness could help to prevent disease from spreading but there was no organised provision of public health. However, as towns grew and public health became more important, the local authorities began to become more active.

The role of war

War was responsible for the Romans settling in Britain. The control that the Romans imposed on much of Europe created prosperity for many and improved communications. In this way, it could be said that war had a positive effect on medicine in Britain, bringing knowledge from Europe. A negative effect of war was the fact that the Druids, who had a good knowledge of using plants in medicine, were suppressed when the Romans settled here.

However, when the Romans left Britain because of war in Europe, society became much more fragmented and public works were allowed to decay. War also disrupted society and trade. People were less likely to travel and exchange knowledge and there were fewer opportunities to build up centres of knowledge and training.

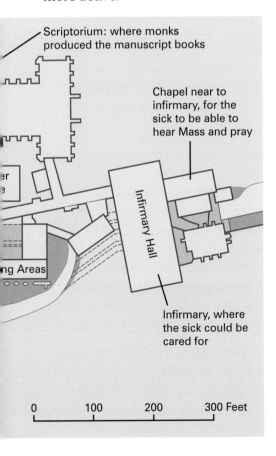

Scriptorium: where monks produced the manuscript books

Chapel near to infirmary, for the sick to be able to hear Mass and pray

Infirmary Hall

Infirmary, where the sick could be cared for

ng Areas

| 0 | 100 | 200 | 300 Feet |

Activities

1 Use Source A to identify as many links between religion and medicine as possible.

2 Use this section (pages 18–29) to draw a spider diagram summarising the ways in which religion affected developments in medicine.

3 Colour code your spider diagram to show (i) the positive aspects of religion's effects on medicine and (ii) ways in which religion held back possible progress in medicine.

4 Explain the problems that faced central government and local authorities when they tried to improve the standard of public health.

5 To what extent was the withdrawal of the Roman army a turning point in medicine in Britain?

Summary

Medicine in Britain has been affected by a range of factors, often acting in combination. These factors have had both positive and negative effects and their importance has varied at different times.

1.12 What makes a source useful to the historian?

What makes a source useful to a historian studying the history of medicine?

The usefulness of a source varies according to what the historian is investigating. So when you are evaluating a source's usefulness, you need to have a clear idea of how the information in the source relates to the historian's enquiry.

For this section of your course, a historian might be interested in:

- ideas from this period about what caused illness and disease
- approaches to public health and the prevention of disease and illness
- how changes in society influenced medicine and public health.

Source A: A scene from the Luttrell Psalter (from c1325–35), a famous medieval manuscript that combines Christian teachings with scenes from everyday life. This illustration is of a doctor drawing blood from a patient.

Look at Source A, which comes from a medieval illuminated manuscript. This source would be more useful for some enquiries than for others.

What caused illness and disease: this source is very useful, it shows Galen's theories on bloodletting in practice.

Approaches to public health: the source is not useful for this enquiry.

Changes in society: the source is useful in showing continuity - doctors still doing in 1325 what Galen had recommended in the second century.

Value of the source

It is important that the historian uses a wide range of sources because all sources have strengths and weaknesses that make them more or less useful.

You should consider whether a source has relevant information but also how that information is affected by the source's reliability, or nature and origins. (Origins means where a source has come from – also called its provenance.)

- What sort of information does the source give and how relevant is it to the enquiry?
- Does the source have any added weight because of its origins or intentions? For example, does it come from someone who was involved in the event it describes or represents?
- If the source gives you only one example, can you assume it is representative of the wider situation? For example, would all doctors at the time have behaved in the same way?

A reliable source is obviously very useful to the historian because it can provide accurate details that can be used to provide an outline of events or to check other sources against. Unfortunately, very few sources are completely reliable.

For early periods like 50AD to 1350, we often know very little about who created a representation like the one in Source A. The sources we have were usually made for very rich people or the Church and represented their views rather than those of ordinary people. Also, because the number of sources we have is quite low, it is difficult to know how representative each one is. There's a fair bit of guesswork involved!

examzone Watch out!

Many students think that the usefulness of a source depends on how much information it contains, or assume that a source produced at the time is automatically better than a source produced later.

Source B: A medieval hospice, showing one man having his back rubbed, another having his hair washed and a man being 'cupped' – when heated glass cups were applied to the skin to draw blood out. The date and origin of this woodcut image are not known.

But unreliable sources are not useless to the historian. Source B is a good example. We don't know anything about its origins, intentions or how representative it is. It almost certainly shows a hospice, which would have been controlled by the Church. Everything about it is fascinating for what it suggests about treatments in the hospice. As long as the historian is clear about the weaknesses of the source, then there is much that a historian could use from this source.

Activities

1 Explain how useful each of the following types of source could be for a historian researching public health in Roman Britain:

   a) archaeological remains, like the Roman Baths in the city of Bath

   b) a Roman law about what should happen when someone is hurt by waste thrown out of a window in Rome

   c) a passage in a book on engineering used across the Empire, that describes the dangers of building houses near swamps

   d) a wall painting from the Italian city of Pompeii showing the different activities available in the public baths

   e) excavated lead pipes used to carry fresh water to people in the British-Roman town of Wroxeter.

2 Study Source B carefully. What do you think the health benefits could be for each of the treatments being shown?

2.1 Medicine and public health c1350–c1750: introduction

32

This section begins with examining medicine and treatment in 1350 before moving on to discover what changed and what remained the same in the period up to 1750. It then examines the public health systems and how these changed or remained the same.

As you study this, you should focus on the key themes about the process of change in medicine and public health. Those key themes are:

- Ideas about the cause and treatment of disease and illness.
- Approaches to public health and prevention of disease and illness.
- The influence of changes in society on medicine and public health.

Before

- Beliefs about what caused disease and therefore how disease was treated in Britain had changed little since Roman times.
- The Romans' sophisticated public health system had long-since collapsed. There were some attempts from the 12th century to try and improve public health in towns.
- The influence of the Church had grown since the collapse of the Roman Empire – the Church controlled education and the training of doctors. Their focus was on caring for the sick, not on curing them.

After

- Not until the late 18th and 19th centuries were there significant advances in the understanding of the causes of ill health and a greater use of science and technology in medicine.

FASCINATING FACT

The fur worn by rich people kept them warm but also tended to attract fleas which carried disease.

 examzone **Watch out!**

Many students assume that life in the Middle Ages was the same for everyone. Remember that there was great variation between different areas of the country and different groups within society.

Anatomy: The structure of the body, for example, bones, nerves, muscles

Apothecary: A person who made medicines and ointments using ingredients such as herbs and spices

Black Death: A highly infectious disease that spread throughout Europe in the mid-14th century

Physiology: The way organs function within the body, for example, the work of the heart, liver and kidneys

Reformation: A period of challenges and divisions within the Christian Church

Renaissance: A period in the 16th and 17th centuries when people thought they were reviving Ancient Greek and Ancient Roman culture but also made new discoveries

Royal Society: A group set up in 1660 to enable educated people to discuss scientific ideas

1348
Black Death reached Britain

1543
Vesalius published *The Fabric of the Human Body*

1628
Harvey published *On the Motion of the Heart and Blood in Animals*

1660
Royal Society established

1665
Plague in London

2.2 What were your chances of a long life if you were born in 1350?

Learning outcome

By the end of this topic you should be able to:

- understand why many people's life expectancy was so low during the Middle Ages

Life expectancy

Nowadays the average life expectancy is around 80 years. In the 1350s it was around 30 years, although the rich, who didn't do manual work and had better diets, might have lived longer. Of course, some individuals lived to be 50, 60 and even 80, but this was unusual.

So what were your chances of a long life? Infant mortality was high. Out of every five children born, there was a high chance that one would die before their first birthday and another would die in childhood. They died from illness, injury, poor living conditions or malnutrition. The remaining three children might grow up and get married and have their own families. Even so, many women died in childbirth and both men and women could die from injuries, while diseases such as smallpox, leprosy and various fevers – called 'agues' – killed people of all ages.

Medicine in the medieval period was focused on dealing with infectious diseases but also on treating daily aches and pains. Conditions that we can now treat successfully, such as heart problems, types of cancer or the need for a hip replacement, were less of a problem because fewer people lived to old age. But when these conditions did develop, there was usually no successful treatment for them.

Source A: A medieval home in 1350. Most people only had one room in their home and during the winter they often brought their animals, such as cows and pigs, indoors.

Activities

1 What clues can you see in the above picture of a peasant's home to suggest reasons why people might become ill?

2 Summarise the reasons why life expectancy in medieval times was so much shorter than it is nowadays, using the following headings: Living conditions; Disease; Other reasons.

3 Explain which of these reasons for a short life expectancy would apply to everyone, and which reasons would apply mainly to the poor.

Challenge

4 How far do you think it is still true that richer people in Britain tend to live longer than poorer people? You should be able to think of points to both support and challenge this idea, and make sure you explain why you find some points are stronger than others.

Summary

Average life expectancy was around 30 years due to illness, injury, poor living conditions and malnutrition.

2.3 Medical ideas and practices at the time of the Black Death

Learning outcomes

By the end of this topic you should be able to:

- understand the range of ideas about causes of the Black Death
- describe the various approaches to preventing and treating it
- explain why people continued to use remedies that did not work

The Black Death

People in medieval times lived in small villages and did not travel far, so epidemics of diseases didn't usually spread over the whole country. However, in 1348, a disease reached England that had already killed thousands of people in Europe. About one-third of the population died from what became known as the **Black Death**.

> Most historians believe that the Black Death was bubonic plague. This was carried by the fleas that lived on black rats; if a flea bit a human, the disease entered the human's bloodstream. As the body tried to fight the illness, the lymph glands swelled into 'buboes'. Other symptoms included fever and chills, headache, vomiting and diarrhea. Of those people who caught the bubonic plague, two out of every three died.

Source A: This Danse Macabre picture shows the understanding that Death could take anyone, at any time.

What did people believe caused the Black Death?

In Europe, in the Middle Ages, most people were Christians and followed the teachings of the Catholic Church. Religion was a very important part of people's lives and part of this was because it provided explanations for bad things that happened. Therefore most people believed that the Black Death was happening because God was displeased with them, or because God was testing them to see if they stayed faithful Christians.

Other ideas about the cause of the plague included:

- an unusual positioning of the planets Mars, Jupiter and Saturn (events among the stars and planets were thought to affect events on Earth)
- poisonous fumes from volcanoes and earthquakes
- bad air (miasma) from decaying refuse, spread through movements in the air
- an imbalance in the Four Humours – most physicians still believed in Galen's theory (see page 13)
- the activities of groups of outsiders, such as strangers or witches (in Europe they also blamed Jews, but the Jews had been forced to leave England the century before this).

How did people try to avoid catching it?

The idea that the plague was a punishment or a test from God meant that groups called 'flagellants' walked in procession to churches, whipping themselves, to show God how sorry they were and to ask for his mercy. Less extreme methods included praying and fasting.

Other actions people tried were:

- carrying herbs and spices to smell
- carrying lucky charms
- smelling bad smells
- tidying the rubbish from the streets
- lighting a fire in the room
- keeping the air moving by ringing bells or keeping birds flying around the room
- not letting people enter the town or village from other places or leaving the area themselves.

How did people treat it?

Some of the actions people tried were:

- praying and holding lucky charms
- eating cool things and taking cold baths
- bloodletting and/or purging
- cutting open the buboes and draining the pus
- holding a piece of bread against the buboes and then burying it in the ground.

Because people in medieval times did not know the true causes of the plague, their treatments and remedies were unlikely to be successful, but some people made a lot of money selling fake potions and remedies!

Others decided to eat, drink and enjoy whatever life they had left.

Source B: A 15th century woodcut. Why did people whip themselves because of the plague?

Activities

1 Explain why, in 1348, someone who caught the plague might go to a priest rather than to a doctor.

2 Why did the plague spread more rapidly in towns than in the countryside? See pages 22–23 for more information.

3 Classify people's ideas about the cause of the plague into:
   a) theories based on belief in the supernatural, such as religion, astrology or witchcraft
   b) ideas based on natural causes, such as unbalanced humours or poisonous gases.

4 Look at the lists of preventions and treatments; explain which actions you think might have been effective and why.

5 Which of the treatments were based on Galen's ideas? Explain the theory behind these treatments.

Challenge

6 Why did people continue to follow the advice of priests and doctors even when so many priests and doctors themselves caught the plague and died?

FASCINATING FACT

The idea that a strong smell could overcome the plague led some people to smell the contents of their toilets every morning.

Summary

There was a range of ideas about the cause of the Black Death. Since these were inaccurate, ideas about its treatment and prevention usually had no effect at all.

2.4 Who was responsible for treating the sick in the Middle Ages?

Learning outcome

By the end of this topic you should be able to:

- understand the range of treatments available during the Middle Ages
- give examples of how different people treated the sick during the Middle Ages

FASCINATING FACT

Some medieval treatments would have worked: for example, honey has antiseptic properties. But hanging a magpie's beak around your neck would probably not have cured your toothache!

Who will you go to?

This poor person is feeling very ill. What choices does she have for treatment?

The trained physician

- has had training at medical school and passed exams
- will diagnose you using your urine and astrological information (see page 21)
- administers treatment based on Galen: likely to be bloodletting, purging to balance your humours or herbal medicine
- consults astrology to determine the best approach to treatment
- can be expensive – you pay for each visit, but he has medical knowledge and believes his treatment to be superior to that of apothecaries and barber-surgeons
- doesn't mix medicines – you get them from the **apothecary**
- might not let blood himself – will direct you to the barber-surgeon
- will be male – women physicians were incredibly rare in this period.

The apothecary

- is trained using passed-down knowledge but has no medical qualifications
- mixes various ingredients to produce medicines or ointments for the physician
- may also make you up their own mixture for a price
- is cheaper than having to consult a physician and then pay an apothecary for the same medicine anyway
- is probably male.

The barber-surgeon

- practises lots of bloodletting; can also pull out rotten teeth and lance boils
- can even have a go at some basic surgery, such as cutting out bladder stones or amputating limbs
- uses no anaesthetics, and has a very low success rate for surgery
- is not trained and is not respected by trained physicians
- can also cut your hair.

Hospital (also see pages 26–27)

- nothing like a modern hospital; usually part of a monastery or convent because Christian values included caring for others
- sick people were usually cared for at home but hospitals looked after the old or those with specific illnesses such as leprosy
- after the **Reformation** in the 16th century some free hospitals were set up in towns, funded by charity.

Housewife-physician (also see pages 48–49)

- knew traditional remedies for things such as sore throats, stomach aches or a temperature
- would also be able to deal with broken bones and with childbirth – may have had a reputation as a local 'wise woman'
- used some remedies based on herbs and other plants, and others based on charms and spells
- could be the lady of the manor, who would treat her servants or families living on manor land.

Prayer and pilgrimage

- Many people would also go on pilgrimage to a holy shrine in the hope that they could be cured of an illness.

Women and medicine

In contrast to in Roman Britain, most treatment was done by women in the home or through local wise women. There were also a few female physicians, such as Trotula, who taught at Salerno medical school in the early 12th century. However, women were not allowed to attend universities, which drove them out of the medical profession by the 14th century. Women continued to work as midwives, but they were expected to have a licence from their bishop to show that they were of good character and would not encourage illegal abortions.

Continuity: the Church and Galen

The dominance of the Church continued throughout the Middle Ages. This meant that most people believed in religious reasons for disease and therefore looked to religion for a cure. Many people would have visited a priest, monk or nun when they became ill. The emphasis was on caring for people – God would cure them if that was what he wanted.

The Church also controlled the majority of education and medical training – most collections of books were in monasteries.

Medical schools were set up at universities during the 12th century, and books such as those by the English doctor John of Gaddesden (c1280–1361) included knowledge from both Muslim and Christian doctors. However, most of a physicians' training was based on Galen's ideas because the Church approved of them (see page 25). Even though a few human dissections were carried out, they were to demonstrate Galen's teaching while his book was read out loud by the lecturer. Nobody was expected to check whether Galen was right or not.

This meant that trained physicians continued to base their diagnosis and treatment on the Four Humours, often using astrology to decide when to bleed a patient. Treatments generally continued to be a mixture of tried and tested herbal remedies, bleeding and purging, and supernatural ideas.

 examzone **Build better answers**

Choose one period and describe the ways in which the Church influenced medicine and treatment:
- the late Middle Ages (6 marks)
- the Renaissance.

 Basic, Level 1
Answers give limited detail about the way in which the Church influenced ideas about the causes of disease and/or care of the sick.

Good, Level 2
Answers describe a variety of the ways in which the Church influenced medicine and treatment through ideas about the cause of disease; control of medical training and acceptance of Galen's ideas without needing to challenge them; caring for the sick through hospitals in convents and monasteries, etc.

Activities

1. Use the information on these pages to create a series of 'Top trumps' cards for each of the different people who cared for the sick. Give each person a rating out of five for (a) their knowledge; (b) their experience; (c) the cost of their treatment; and (d) likely success rate.

2. Explain why the housewife-physician was less respected than the physician, even though she treated more people.

3. Draw an ideas map to explain how religion was linked to medicine at this time. Use the headings: Ideas about the causes of ill health; Treatment and prevention of ill health; Care for the sick; Medical training.

Summary

There were many different choices of health treatment for the rich, but very few for the poor. There were few new treatments as there were few new ideas about the causes of disease.

2.5 The impact of the Medical Renaissance (c1500–c1750)

Learning outcome

By the end of this topic you should be able to:

- understand the impact of the Renaissance on reducing the influence of the Church and bringing a scientific approach to medicine
- describe the work of Vesalius and Harvey and explain why it had limited impact on medical treatment

Renaissance and Reformation

Renaissance means 'rebirth' and it describes a period in European history when Ancient Greek and Roman ideas became fashionable again. It was also a time when European exploration in Africa and the Americas led to new attitudes and a search for knowledge. Meanwhile, changes in religion known as the Reformation led to a decline in the Church's authority, even though most people remained very strongly religious.

A new attitude to knowledge began to spread. Instead of relying on the views of an accepted 'authority', educated people wanted to check knowledge for themselves. This led to a scientific approach of testing and recording details, then sharing these results with other people.

A group meeting in London formed themselves into the **Royal Society** in 1660, with King Charles II's approval and support. The society had its own laboratory and the latest scientific equipment so members could experiment and show their discoveries. The Royal Society published regular accounts of their discussions and findings on a wide range of scientific theories. This helped to spread the new ideas.

New inventions

This scientific approach led to new technology, such as mechanisms in pumps and clocks, that helped people accept the idea of the body functioning as a machine. When the Dutch scientist Antonie van Leeuwenhoek developed better lenses for a microscope, he discovered bacteria, which he described as 'animalcules' in a letter to the Royal Society in 1673.

Perhaps the most important invention, however, was the printing press. This meant that printed copies of books and journals could be produced quickly and cheaply and physicians could learn from each other's research and experiments. Meanwhile, the printing press also produced herbals, which described plants and herbal remedies. These were printed in ordinary language instead of Latin.

Vesalius, Harvey and new ideas about the body

In 1543, Andreas Vesalius, the Professor of Surgery at Padua University in Italy, published an important book called *The Fabric of the Human Body*. This included drawings showing the muscles, nerves, organs and skeleton of the human body based on dissections of corpses. Carrying out human dissections also meant that Vesalius discovered some of Galen's teachings were wrong.

Working through experiments and observation, William Harvey, an Englishman, also found errors in Galen's ideas. He published an explanation of his ideas, supported by details of his studies, in a book in 1628 called *An Anatomical Account of the Motion of the Heart and Blood in Animals*.

Source A: An illustration from Vesalius' book showing the muscles of the human body.

Galen	Vesalius
Said the heart is divided by a septum which has holes in it to allow blood to pass through.	Showed the septum does not have holes.
Said the liver had five parts or lobes.	Showed the liver does not have any lobes.
Said the lower jaw was made up of two bones.	Showed this was true for monkeys and pigs but the lower jaw in humans is a single bone.
Said the sternum had seven parts.	Showed it only had three.

Galen	Harvey
Said veins carry a mixture of blood and air.	Showed that veins only carry blood.
Said that blood is constantly manufactured by the liver and used up as it travels around the body.	Showed that blood circulates repeatedly around the body, with the heart acting as the pump.

The impact on medical treatment

Vesalius and Harvey used scientific methods to investigate how the body works. This had a positive impact on medicine as more physicians began to use a scientific approach to diagnosing and treating people (see pages 40–41). However, it took over 40 years before Harvey's ideas were accepted by other doctors and taught at medical schools. This is because people are often reluctant to accept new ideas, especially as doctors' training was still based on Galen's ideas and most physicians did not carry out dissections themselves.

Furthermore, Harvey's work was on physiology (how the body's organs function) rather than on the cause or treatment of illness, and so his work did not seem particularly relevant to the work of physicians and the problems of disease.

FASCINATING FACT

Harvey carried out post-mortems on his father and his sister.

Activities

1 Explain why the invention of the printing press at this time was so important for the work of Vesalius and Harvey.

2 Produce a newspaper front page reporting on Harvey's ideas.

 exam**zone**

Build better answers

Why did the discoveries of the Renaissance have such limited impact on the understanding and treatment of disease? (12 marks)
You may use the following in your answer:
• Doctor's training
• William Harvey
You must also include information of your own.

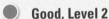

■ **Basic, Level 1**
Answers offer general comments with little detail.

● **Good, Level 2**
Answers contain details of Renaissance discoveries or medical treatments.

▲ **Excellent, Level 3**
Answers contain accurate details of discoveries and show these had little impact on medical treatment as they did not develop an understanding of what causes illness. May also explore other aspects, e.g. the influence of the Church.

Summary

The Medical Renaissance brought new ideas about **anatomy** and **physiology**, and the printing press spread these ideas faster than before. But there was resistance to change, and few developments in understanding disease.

2.6 Doctors and training

Learning outcomes

By the end of this topic you should be able to:

● understand the impact of the Renaissance on the training of some doctors

● explain the importance of the work of John Hunter as an example of the impact of this training, as seen in his later career

● understand that treatment was still very limited at this time

The impact of the Renaissance on doctors' training

The diagram shows what affected the training of doctors in this period.

Improved technology, e.g. thermometers, microscopes, etc.

Improved knowledge of anatomy and physiology through books such as those by Vesalius and Harvey.

What affected the training of doctors?

Growing acceptance that physicians should do dissections of the human body for themselves.

Introduction of some medical schools and teaching hospitals.

Growing importance of a scientific approach – observation of symptoms and experiment with treatments.

Source A: This picture, by Hogarth, drawn in 1751, shows a scene in a dissecting room at the Surgeon's Hall.

examzone
Build better answers

How useful is this picture to a historian who is investigating the training of doctors in the 18th century? Use Source A and your own knowledge to explain your answer.   (8 marks)

■ **Basic, Level 1**
Answers assume the source is useful because it is from the time and shows an aspect of doctors' training.

● **Good, Level 2**
Answers contain analysis of the source to show why it may or may not be useful or an analysis of the nature, purpose and origins of the source to assess how reliable and therefore important it is.

▲ **Excellent, Level 3**
As for Level 2, plus answers use their own knowledge to assess how representative the source is, showing that this contributes to knowledge of the training of some doctors.

Improved training

More physicians travelled to universities in Europe or Edinburgh for medical training. Training began to take on a more practical role, observing and examining patients, rather than just reading books. Students also began to take part in dissections themselves. Some physicians even began to set up their own medical schools.

John Hunter – a scientific approach

John Hunter was trained in the new Renaissance methodology and his later career shows the impact of these ideas on medicine and training. Why was Hunter important?

- His lectures on anatomy helped to develop a more professional approach to medical training.
- He emphasised the importance of observation and experiment.
- His students included Edward Jenner (see page 54), who followed Hunter's methods when investigating cowpox.
- He employed a secretary to write up his notes and paid an artist to draw the discoveries he made through dissection.
- He published several important works, including one about the changes that occurred in pregnancy.
- John and his elder brother William, set up their own medical school in London where physicians received intense training.

Source B: One of the illustrations from Hunter's work on pregnancy.

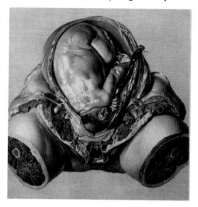

Activities

1   Look at the ideas map on page 40. Which do you think was the most important aspect of changes in medical training during this period and why?

2   Explain why the changes in medical training had little impact on doctors' ability to cure disease.

FASCINATING FACT

Hunter had an extension built to his house so that he could display all his specimens. Part of the extension had to be open to a height of two storeys so that he could display the stuffed body of a giraffe.

Source C: John Hunter, 1728–1793.

Extremely skilled in the techniques used in dissection, an intensely curious man and a workaholic.

Studied many aspects of anatomy, using specimens to show the human body's structure and physiology, the medical problems of conditions like arthritis and also the progressive stages of a disease.

Built up a huge collection of human and animal specimens.

Carried out various experiments as part of a study on the sexually transmitted infections of syphilis and gonorrhoea.

Summary

The Renaissance sparked advances in knowledge of the body and emphasised a more scientific approach to diagnosing and treating disease. This began to improve doctors' training, the impact of which can be seen towards the end of the 18th century, although doctors still had limited ability to treat disease.

2.7 Public health 1350–1750: the problems

Learning outcomes

By the end of this topic you should be able to:

- describe the increasing public health problems in towns
- give reasons why it was difficult to deal with the public health problems in towns

As towns grew bigger during the medieval period, public health provision became a bigger problem too. Some attempts were made to deal with these problems:

- Some local authorities paid for piped water supplies and sewer systems.
- Some towns had public baths, called stewes, where people bathed together in large wooden tubs.
- Richer people might have their own latrines, which ran into a cesspit.
- Some towns had public latrines so people did not need to relieve themselves in the street.

Medieval people were aware that there was a connection between dirt and disease, even if they couldn't explain it. The town councils passed by-laws ordering people to keep the streets clean and fined people who broke the rules. However, no one expected the local authorities to organize the removal of rubbish, and people had to pay for their cesspits to be emptied. In the same way, no one expected the king and central government to make laws about public health or to increase taxes, and therefore many of the improvements that happened were paid for by local individuals.

Case study: how could London get clean water?

In the 13th century, lead pipes were laid to bring water from the river Tyburn to London, and people would go to the pool of water at the end of the conduit (channel) to collect water. There were also water sellers who came through the streets, but the water was usually taken from a polluted river so most people drank ale rather than water.

Source A: The 'Little Conduit' at Cheapside. Water from the River Tyburn could be collected from the pool inside the building; this water was cleaner than water taken from the River Thames and was free to those who went to collect it.

Although London's council recognised the need for clean water, it could not decide what to do about it because it knew people would oppose any increases in their local taxes. Luckily two men were prepared to use their own money to improve the situation.

> In 1602 Edmund Colthurst suggested constructing an artificial river to bring water to London over a 38-mile journey from the River Lee in Hertfordshire.

> The project relied on gravity to get the water to London, the route had to be carefully planned in order to ensure that the channels always led downwards and the water would keep flowing.

> Colthurst only managed to complete two miles due to financial difficulties.

> Sir Hugh Myddleton revived this idea in 1609 and offered to pay for the work himself.

> There were many protests from landowners along the route.

> Myddleton had King James I's support – and James even paid half the costs.

> The project was finished in 1613.

The project's completion meant that fresh water was available in parts of north-east London, but the supply could not keep up with the growing population of the city. Although some people continued to get their water from wells or water sellers, by 1750 most water was supplied by private companies, either piped to the house or available at standpipes on street corners, which were turned on at set times each day.

Sanitation: chamber pots and water closets

Although there were several attempts to improve access to water, there was little recognition of the need to improve sanitation. This had the effect of creating health risks, especially when sewage polluted the water. In medieval towns, toilets were usually wooden seats above a cesspit, and people wiped themselves with leaves or moss. Several families might share one cesspit and ashes might be scattered over the sewage to keep the smell down, but it needed to be cleaned out regularly. These sorts of toilets were called earth closets.

Inside the house, most people used chamber pots, which were emptied into the drain in the middle of the street – or sometimes the contents were just thrown into the streets from an upstairs window.

Source B: Sanitation in the Middle Ages, from an old wood cut.

The situation was not much better for the rich. The king had a 'close stool', which was a padded seat over a large bucket, and the most important job within Henry VIII's private rooms was the Groom of the Stool – the man in charge of the king's chamber pot! (One of his jobs was to wipe the royal bottom!) Meanwhile, at Hampton Court there was a 'great house of easement', which had 28 seats arranged on two levels. The waste emptied into brick-lined drains and then into the River Thames.

When Sir John Harrington invented a water closet (WC) in 1596, using water to flush away the sewage, Queen Elizabeth I liked the idea so much that she had a WC installed at Richmond Palace but many people ridiculed the idea and the WC did not develop properly until 200 years later.

> **FASCINATING FACT**
>
> Toilet paper was first used in Britain in 1857. It was sold by chemists – but it was not on display because people were embarrassed to see it, so it was kept under the counter. Toilet rolls were first sold in 1928. Soft paper was introduced in 1932 but was unpopular at first.

Activities

1 Write a letter to parliament in the 16th century trying to persuade them to pass a law to make all towns provide piped water, toilets and sewers.

2 What factors (i) helped and (ii) hindered the attempts to improve London's water supply?

3 To what extent did public health provision improve between 1350 and 1750?

Summary

In the medieval and Renaissance periods, public health became a problem for local authorities as towns grew bigger. There were some improvements in the provision of clean water but it was not organised or paid for by local or central authorities and there was little change in methods for dealing with sewage. At this time, the link between hygiene and health was not very clear.

2.8 Public health 1350–1750: government action

44

Learning outcomes

By the end of this topic you should be able to:

- understand the problems the authorities faced when dealing with public health issues
- understand the factors affecting the way authorities dealt with public health issues
- evaluate the role of central government and local authorities in dealing with public health issues

In the Renaissance period, some cities and towns became very large; for example, London had a population of about 100,000 and, in these conditions, infectious diseases were difficult to control. During an epidemic, local authorities often ordered a cleanup and might order barrels of tar to be burned in the streets to purify the air, while the king and central government might order a day of prayer. However, these measures would have little effect.

FASCINATING FACT

Henry VIII was particularly worried over an outbreak of 'the sweating sickness' at his court in 1528, which had a high death rate. He immediately fled London and moved constantly to new residences, taking only a few people with him, including his best physician – his second best physician was sent to treat Anne Boleyn, who had caught the disease.

The Great Plague, 1665

In 1665 a disease struck London that killed about a quarter of its population. This disease was bubonic plague – the same disease that historians think caused the Black Death in the 14th century. This time there were major differences in how the outbreak was dealt with, although methods of treating the disease hadn't really changed. In 1348, individuals and communities tried to prevent the plague from spreading; in 1665, there was a lot of pressure on the town authorities to take on this role. Laws were passed to try to contain the disease.

Source A: There were several outbreaks of plague throughout the 16th and 17th centuries, but the most famous of these epidemics was in London in 1665, shown in this contemporary pamphlet.

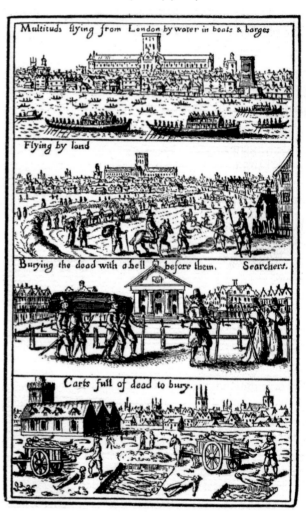

- They closed the theatres to prevent crowds gathering and banned large funerals.
- Dogs and cats were killed.
- Barrels of tar were burned in the streets.
- Carts came through the city daily to collect the dead bodies and bury them at night in large mass graves deep in the ground.
- If a case of plague was discovered, the whole household were boarded up in their house for 28 days and a red cross was painted on the door together with the words 'Lord have mercy on us'.
- Days of fasting and prayers were ordered.

Most of these measures were ineffective and many people, including King Charles II, left the city. Even isolation and **quarantine** did not work because the disease was not spread by human contact but was carried by the fleas on the rats. Until Pasteur's work led to a better understanding of disease in the 19th century, neither doctors nor governments could deal effectively with infectious diseases such as the plague.

The problem of gin

The role of government is important in public health provision because only government has the power to pass laws to bring about changes. This is illustrated in the ways the authorities tried to deal with the Great Plague but can also be seen in the government's response to the problem of gin.

Source B: This picture titled 'Gin Lane' was painted in 1751 by William Hogarth. It warns of the dangers of gin.

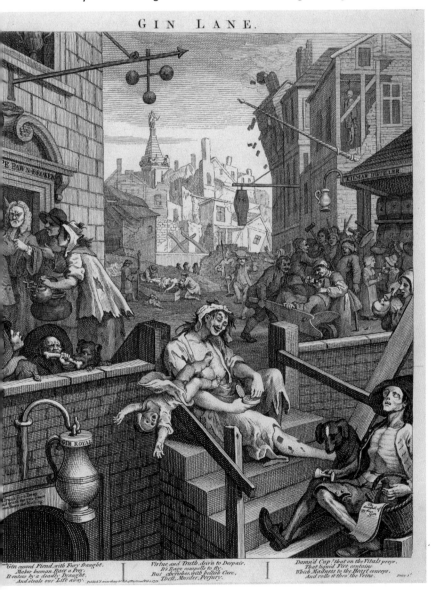

GIN LANE.

There was public concern in the 18th century that cheap gin was having a bad effect on the poor. This is shown in the picture (Source B) by the artist Hogarth: the scene in Gin Lane suggests that strong alcohol has a bad effect on society. In 1750, the government passed laws that made gin more expensive. This was partly to try to improve the standard of health among the poor but also because the government was concerned about the effect on the economy if people were too drunk to work properly. The increase in price also helped to reduce the death rate from excessive drinking.

Activities

1 Compare the responses of the authorities to the Black Death (on pages 34–35) and the Great Plague in 1665. In what ways were they similar and different?

2 Make a list of the ways in which (i) the king and central government and (ii) local authorities dealt with infectious diseases such as the plague. For each method explain how effective it would have been.

3 Why do you think central government did not raise taxes or pass new laws to improve the public health situation more often?

4 How far did the tax on gin show the government taking on a new, preventive role in medicine?

Summary

As the population of towns grew and the living conditions became more crowded, disease spread easily. However, until Pasteur's germ theory, people did not understand how infectious diseases were spread and therefore the attempts of local authorities to deal with epidemics often failed. Central government rarely got involved in public health issues until the 19th century.

2.9 Change and continuity: how much did medicine change between 1350 and 1750?

Learning outcomes

By the end of this topic you should be able to:

- identify examples of both change and continuity within this period
- understand that there were elements of change and continuity in medicine simultaneously throughout this period
- analyse the role of various factors in developments during this period

Renaissance developments

Before 1500, nearly all people were Catholic and followed the teachings of the Catholic Church. We have seen how people started to challenge and test existing beliefs and this was true of religious ideas as well. By 1600, people belonged to many different Churches, which held slightly different beliefs and taught different things. This meant there was no longer the one hugely dominant Church that controlled society. As the influence of the Church declined, its grip on education and beliefs about what caused illness declined too.

This had an impact on medical training as some doctors did not just accept the traditional theories that people had been taught. It helped lead to the significant changes in people's knowledge and understanding of the human body during the Renaissance period.

However, it would be a mistake to think that religion was no longer a huge part of most people's lives or that it stopped their belief that God was the cause, and therefore potential cure, of disease. Many people, including many doctors, stuck to the same ideas and beliefs.

When there was a plague epidemic in London in 1665, the treatments used were similar to those used in 1348. Ordinary medical treatment continued to be based on the Four Humours. People also believed that a king's touch could cure them of tuberculosis (TB). Charles II (1630–1685) touched over 8,000 sufferers of the disease in one year.

Here are some events and factors affecting the development of medicine during this period:

The Church controlled education and medical training.

The Church discouraged dissection.

Herbal remedies were passed down from one generation to the next.

Universities and medical schools were founded in the 12th century.

Some herbal remedies worked.

New plants were discovered when new lands were explored.

The microscope was invented.

The works of Galen were used as the basis for all medical training.

The authority of the Catholic Church decreased.

Many people were reluctant to change the way they did things.

The mechanical pump was invented.

The printing press was invented.

Some people felt better after being bled or purged.

Few people could afford to go to a trained physician.

Many people believed that their lives were affected by supernatural events.

Most minor illnesses and injuries were treated by the women in the family.

Source A: A 1505 woodcut showing an apothecary instructing his assistant in the use of various remedies.

Activities

1 Study the list of events and factors affecting developments in medicine on the opposite page.

   Classify them into two groups:

   a) points leading to progress

   b) points holding back developments so that old ideas continued.

2 Do you think that the period from 1350 to 1750 was a period in medicine of mainly change or mainly continuity (continuing old methods)? Explain your answer.

3 How would your answer to question 2 have been different if the question was about the time period 1350–1500 or 1500–1700? Explain your answer.

4 Go back to the two lists you made in your answer to question 1. Colour code your lists to show:

   • the role of religion and beliefs

   • scientific knowledge

   • technological equipment

   • social attitudes.

5 Which of these four factors do you think has been most important in leading to change and which has been most important in maintaining continuity?

examzone
Build better answers

How far do you agree that the period between 1350 and 1750 was one of continuity rather than change in medicine? Explain your answer. (16 marks)

You may use the following in your answer:

• The Renaissance

• Herbal remedies and Galen's theories

You must also include information of your own.

 Basic, Level 1

Answers offer general statements on things that changed or stayed the same. For example, *'people relied on the same treatments and most couldn't afford to go to a doctor'*.

Good, Level 2

Answers offer description of some changes and/or aspects of continuity. For example, describing the discoveries of Vesalius and Harvey and outlining that treatment remained largely the same.

 Better, Level 3

Answers offer analysis as well as description, with support from relevant material. For example, analysing the amount of change resulting from Renaissance discoveries.

 Excellent, Level 4

Answers describe and analyse the amount of change and continuity across different aspects of medicine such as treatment, medical training and ideas about the causes of disease before making a judgement on whether there was more continuity or change. Will be well-supported by accurate material.

Make sure you write accurately – there are three extra marks available for spelling, grammar and punctuation in these questions.

Summary

There were some important changes in knowledge of the body during this period but there was also a great deal of continuity, especially in the ideas about illness and the medical treatments that were used.

2.10 A lack of sources – the role of women in medicine 1350–1750

Researching the role of women

The role of women in medieval medicine is a difficult topic to research because our evidence is so limited. Most people in the period 1350–1750 could not read and write, and although boys might receive an education to become lawyers or merchants, the education for girls (even in wealthy families) was based around running a home. This means that we have very few sources produced by women to tell us about their lives in the medieval period.

Furthermore, the accounts written by men tended to focus on events such as new laws, wars and the actions of the rich. They did not feel that accounts of daily life were important, and we therefore have only a limited amount of sources to tell us about family life and women's activities.

What do these pictures suggest about the role of women in medieval medicine?

Many women made their own herbal remedies.

Women were usually responsible for the health of the family.

A midwife and female attendant would help a woman through childbirth.

Sometimes we can gather together information from different sources and try to build up a picture of women during the medieval period, but we do not know whether the women in these sources are examples of typical behaviour or unusual cases.

Source A: The legal records of a court case in Paris in 1322.

> Jacoba visited the sick folk, examining their urine, touching, feeling and holding their pulses, body and limbs. After this examination she would say to the sick folk 'I will cure you by God's will, if you will trust in me', making a compact with them and receiving money from them.

This legal record describes how the city's university accused a woman called Jacoba of working without the proper qualifications. A number of people gave evidence that her treatments had been successful and it was suggested that the only reason Jacoba was prosecuted was because she was so successful that male doctors were losing business.

Source B: The Paston family wrote many letters to each other in the 14th century and these include comments about daily illnesses and injuries. Here is an extract from a letter from Margaret Paston. (Treacle or syrup was expected to remove infections.)

> I ask you heartily that you will quickly send me a pot of treacle for I have used that which I had. One of the tallest young men in this parish lies sick and has a great fever. I have sent my Uncle Berney the pot of treacle that you bought for him.

Source C: Lady Grace Mildmay was from a wealthy English family in the 16th century and there are a number of recipes for herbal medicines listed in her papers. Here she is writing about headaches.

> If it arises from phlegm, the face will be full and pale, and the eyes swollen and dark. For remedy of the headache, of what kind soever it be, according to the signs of the offending humour, apply cordials or coolers inward and outward. If giddiness or other grief in the head have been occasioned by keeping corrupt fluids within the body, then must opening things be given.

Source D: In a book he wrote in 1651, Dr James Primrose complained about women going beyond their proper responsibilities and doing the work of a physician.

> They know how to make a bed well, boyle pottage, and they know many remedies for diseases. But [dealing with ulcers and wounds] can only be known by a skilful physician and women ought not to meddle with them. They take their remedies out of English books but Galen teaches that remedies should be altered according to the person, place, part affected and other circumstances and seeing that these things cannot be attained without much labour and study, I cannot be brought to believe women are able to understand, or perform what they promise.

Source E: Here is an extract from a letter from John Paston to his wife, Margery.

> Send as quickly as possible a large plaster (poultice) for the king's attorney for an ache in his knees. When you send me the plaster you must write to me telling me how long it should stay on the knee. And whether he must wrap any cloth around the plaster to keep it warm.

Activities

1 How much can the historian generalise about the role of women in medicine in the period c1350–c1750 from individual examples (such as the three women – Jacoba, Margaret Paston and Lady Grace Mildmay – named in the sources in this section)?

2 How much weight should the historian put on the complaints of Dr Primrose in Source D?

3 Is it reasonable for historians to generalize about the situation of women when we have only a few pieces of surviving evidence spread over a long period of time? Explain your answer.

4 How do you think the historian can deal with the problems caused by the lack of sources about medieval women?

3.1 Medicine and public health c1750–c1900: introduction

This section begins with examining the situation in 1750 before moving on to discover what changed and what remained the same in the period up to 1900. As you study this, you should focus on the key themes about the process of change in medicine and public health. Those key themes are:

- ideas about the cause and treatment of disease and illness
- approaches to public health and prevention of disease and illness
- the influence of changes in society on medicine and public health.

Before...

In the medieval and Renaissance periods, people did not know what caused diseases to spread, and medical treatment was based on theories such as the Four Humours or miasma (bad air). During the Reformation in the 16th century, the influence of the Church on medical training and treatment began to decline, while a better understanding of the body began to develop, based on a more scientific approach to knowledge and understanding.

After...

In the modern period, the role of science and technology improved our ability to diagnose and treat illness, but there was also an emphasis on prevention of illness through **vaccinations**, genetic research and changes in lifestyle. Women became far more involved in professional medicine, and the government took on a wide range of responsibilities within public health.

Epidemic: A severe outbreak of an infectious disease

Industrial: Connected to industry and manufacturing

Industrial revolution: The period c1750–1900 when there were rapid changes in the way work and industry was organised

Inoculation: A way of giving a patient a mild dose of an illness so that the body builds up its immunity

Miasma: The theory that disease is caused by poisonous vapours in the air

Spontaneous generation: The idea that rubbish or decaying material creates microbes (small organisms or germs)

Vaccination: A safe way of stimulating the body's immune system against a particular disease

1796
Edward Jenner tested his vaccination for smallpox

1801
The first population census in Britain

1831
Cholera first arrived in Britain

1842
Chadwick's report

1848
Public Health Act

1858
General Medical Act

1859
Florence Nightingale published her *Notes on Nursing*

1861
Louis Pasteur published his germ theory

1865
New sewer system for London completed

1875
Public Health Act

3.2 How did the industrial revolution affect health?

Learning outcome

By the end of this topic you should be able to:

● understand the effect of changes in industry on medicine and health

Source A: A picture showing a typical industrial town.

The term '**industrial revolution**' is used to describe this period because it was a time of great changes in the way people worked and this led to great changes in the way they lived.

In the mid-18th century various machines were invented that were powered by water or steam and could work more quickly and efficiently than manual workers. The use of machinery in agriculture meant that there was less work to do in the countryside and therefore many people moved to the rapidly growing towns (such as Manchester and Leeds) to work in the new factories. In these towns, the standard of workers' health was usually very poor and disease spread quickly.

● The conditions in the factories led to ill health, for example, poor ventilation created breathing problems.
● There were often accidents in the factories from the machinery.
● The housing in the towns was of poor quality and rooms were damp and poorly ventilated.
● Living conditions were cramped, with a house often containing more than one family.
● Sewers often ran into the rivers where people got their 'clean' water.
● In the big towns and cities there was less access to fresh food than in rural areas (see page 42 for more information on public health).

examzone
Watch out!

Many students assume that everyone quickly accepted new scientific ideas. Remember that new ideas are often accepted very slowly and that people had to pay for medical care; this meant that many of the developments in this period had very limited impact on the lives and health of ordinary people.

Activities

1 Look at the tombstones on page 50 showing details taken from a report that was published in 1842. What things can you tell about life expectancy in this period from the details on these tombstones?

2 Look at Source A above and make a list of all the things that would make people unhealthy.

Summary

Poor standards of public health in the industrial towns led to a low life expectancy among workers.

As you saw with the Renaissance period, historians find it convenient to use labels for different periods, even though they are not very precise.

3.3 Killer diseases in Britain, c1750-c1900

Learning outcomes

By the end of this topic you should be able to:

- give reasons why there was a high mortality rate in industrial towns
- understand why people's ideas about the causes of disease seemed appropriate

Ideas about the causes of disease c1750–c1900

During the Renaissance there had been a growing interest in science. This affected people's ideas about the causes of disease, and by the 18th century they were less likely to blame disease on supernatural causes or unbalanced Humours. People had always been aware that disease spread quickly in dirty, smelly and unhygienic conditions, and so the search for a new explanation of illness based on natural causes now developed into two main theories:

- **miasma**: disease was caused by bad air that was filled with poisonous fumes from rotting matter
- **spontaneous generation**: disease was caused by germs that were produced by flesh and vegetables as they rotted.

These theories came to prominence as killer diseases in Britain reached new heights.

FASCINATING FACT

In 1842 an investigation into housing in Bury, in Lancashire, found that 63 families slept five or more people in one bed and 210 families slept four in a bed. Another investigation into housing in London found that, in one ordinary courtyard, 120 people shared one toilet.

The growth in urban populations 1801–1851

During the industrial revolution, in the late 18th and early 19th centuries, the population of industrial towns grew rapidly. Housing for factory workers was often of very poor quality and many families could only afford to live in a single room. In these conditions, disease spread rapidly, especially as there was poor sanitation and limited access to water.

Population	1801 (thousands)	1851 (thousands)
Glasgow	77	329
Liverpool	82	376
Birmingham	71	233
Manchester	70	303
Leeds	53	172
London	957	2,362

Source A: An engraving of London in the mid-19th century showing the crowded and unhygienic conditions in which most people lived.

Killer diseases

More information on the killer diseases in industrial Britain is given in this chart:

Disease	How it is spread	Effects
Cholera	Through bacteria passed on through food and water that have been contaminated by the excreta of an infected person.	Sickness and severe diarrhoea; sufferer dies from dehydration, often within 24 hours. Up to two-thirds of sufferers died.
Diphtheria	Through tiny droplets when coughing and sneezing or through contact with the soiled clothing of an infected person.	Bleeding and sometimes paralysis; suffocation from a blocked throat often leads to death. The death rate was one in ten but it particularly affected children and survivors took a long time to recover.
Smallpox	By touch, or through tiny droplets when coughing or sneezing.	A rash turns into blisters filled with pus; the blisters become crusted and fall off, leaving deep scars. About a third of sufferers died.
Tuberculosis (TB; also called consumption)	Through tiny droplets when coughing and sneezing.	Coughing becomes constant; victim brings up blood; chest pains; often severe weight loss. Nearly half of sufferers died.
Typhoid	Through bacteria passed on through food and water that have been contaminated by the excreta of an infected person or through food infected by flies.	Headaches, fever, constipation and then severe diarrhoea. Up to one-third of sufferers died, especially those who were already weak, such as the old, the young, the malnourished.

exam zone

Summary

Epidemics of infectious diseases killed many people, especially in the towns, where diseases spread quickly. Although diseases such as plague and leprosy had almost died out, new diseases such as cholera, were extremely frightening.

3.4 The fight against smallpox

Learning outcomes

- understand why people used inoculation and the problems associated with it
- describe Jenner's work on creating a vaccine for smallpox and explain why he was opposed
- explain the factors that made the smallpox vaccination successful

Inoculation

If you catch a disease, your body creates special cells called antibodies to fight off the infection and, if you survive, you may become immune to any further attacks of that disease. The fact that some people survived several epidemics of the plague or smallpox was accepted by people throughout history even though they could not explain why it happened. This practical knowledge led to a procedure called **inoculation**, which was developed in China and spread through Asia.

1 A small amount of pus is taken from a sufferer's smallpox blister.

2 It is spread into a small cut made between the thumb and forefinger of the person being inoculated.

3 A mild version of smallpox develops; the person survives and is then immune to further attacks.

> **FASCINATING FACT**
> Inoculation in Britain was tested on condemned prisoners in 1723.

Lady Mary Wortley Montagu (the wife of the British ambassador to Turkey) witnessed this procedure in Turkey in the early 18th century. She had nearly died from smallpox when she was younger and as she was keen to protect her children she had them inoculated in 1721.

The idea quickly became very popular in Britain, and people would even have smallpox parties where they would all be inoculated together. Since doctors were paid for this, they could make a lot of money. However, inoculation did not completely solve the problem of smallpox because not everyone could afford to have it done and inoculation was not always effective or safe.

Activities

1 Study the points in the box on Jenner's work opposite and write them out as three lists:

a) one showing all the good points about Jenner's own work

b) one showing all the reasons why there was opposition to Jenner's work

c) one showing outside events that affected Jenner's work.

2 Look carefully at the 1802 cartoon. How does it suggest that people did not like the idea of being given cowpox to inoculate against smallpox?

Source A: Cartoon produced in 1802. The caption says 'The Cow Pock – or – the Wonderful Effects of the New Inoculation'

1807

19th Century News
Doctor from Gloucestershire gets £20,000 payout

Edward Jenner, a doctor in Gloucestershire, was surprised when local people said they did not need to be inoculated. They claimed that if they had already had cowpox they would not catch smallpox. Jenner decided to check this idea and carried out tests on an eight-year-old boy called James Phipps.

'On 14 May 1796, I took some cowpox matter from a blister on the arm of Sarah Nelmes and inserted it into two cuts I had made on James's arm,' said Jenner. 'A week later he became chilly, lost his appetite and had a headache but the next day he was completely well. On 1 July I injected him with smallpox matter but no disease followed. Several months later I tried again, but he still didn't develop even a mild case of smallpox!'

To make absolutely sure of his findings, Jenner injected another 23 people in this way (including his eleven-month-old son) and in 1798 he decided to publish his ideas, giving the name 'vaccination' to his new technique (because vacca is the Latin for cow). However, the Royal Society refused to publish his account and he had to pay for his report to be printed himself. In 1802 the British government awarded Jenner £10,000 for his work against smallpox – and now, five years later, they have given him an additional £20,000.

Jenner's work

- Jenner worked in a scientific way and did a number of tests.
- Jenner had pamphlets printed for other scientists to read; the pamphlets described his experiments very clearly so that the other scientists could check his work.
- Jenner's discovery showed that it was possible to prevent some people catching a disease.
- Jenner could not explain how the link between cowpox and smallpox worked. The link only existed between smallpox and cowpox. It did not work for any other diseases.
- The procedure was not always successful, and some people did develop smallpox because some doctors did not carry it out carefully enough.
- Jenner did not mind other people using his ideas – he wanted lots of people to benefit from his work.
- In 1802, the Jennerian Society was set up in London to promote vaccination and within two years over 12,000 people had been vaccinated.
- When the government provided a grant to pay for people to have free vaccinations, doctors lost money because people no longer paid for inoculations. Therefore many doctors opposed Jenner's work.
- Napoleon in France and President Jefferson in the USA both thought vaccination was a great breakthrough.
- In 1852, the government made it compulsory to be vaccinated.
- When the British government enforced compulsory vaccination in 1871, the number of smallpox cases dropped dramatically, and in 1979 the World Health Organization announced that smallpox had been wiped out completely.

Activities

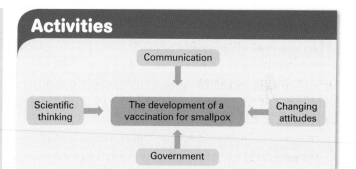

3 The diagram above shows four factors that affected the development of a vaccine for smallpox. Make a copy of this diagram and use the points in the box on Jenner's work to provide examples of the role of each factor.

4 'Individuals and their discoveries are not enough on their own to bring about medical progress.' Explain how far you think this statement applies to Jenner and his work.

Challenge

5 Go back to the list of killer diseases on page 53. Research when a vaccination was successfully discovered for each of them and plot them on a timeline.

Summary

Jenner's promotion of innoculation was an important way of preventing smallpox, but his methods could not be applied to other infectious diseases.

3.5 The development of the germ theory and vaccination

Learning outcomes

By the end of this topic you should be able to:

- understand how the development of the germ theory was an important breakthrough in the development of vaccines and laid the foundations for later work on the treatment and prevention of disease

Source A: Pasteur in his laboratory.

Scientific experiments

Technology

Recording and communicating results of experiments

The germ theory

In the 1850s Louis Pasteur, a French chemist, investigated the problem of liquids turning sour in the brewing and vinegar industries.

More powerful microscopes had recently become available, which meant Pasteur could observe the growth of unwanted small organisms in the liquids.

He discovered heating the liquid killed the bacteria and stopped the liquid going sour.

In 1861, Pasteur published his germ theory, showing that there were microbes in the air and that they caused decay. His work proved the idea of spontaneous generation was wrong because no decay happened if matter was placed in a sealed container. This showed that the microbes causing decay were not produced from the matter itself but were in the air around it.

In 1875, Robert Koch, a German doctor who had read Pasteur's work, decided to investigate whether bacteria were linked to disease. Working with a team of scientists, and funded by the German government, Koch identified the specific microbes that caused the disease anthrax in sheep.

In 1879, Pasteur's research team was studying chicken cholera microbes and injecting chickens with the disease. A culture of the bacteria was accidentally left on one side and when it was used, a couple of weeks later, it had become a weakened version, which didn't harm the chickens. Pasteur realised that this could be used as a vaccine to create immunity from that disease for chickens. He called this process 'vaccination' in tribute to the importance of Jenner's work.

Koch identified the microbes causing TB in 1882 and those causing cholera in 1883.

Koch found that chemical dyes could be used to stain specific bacteria so they could be studied more easily under the microscope.

The significance of germ theory

Pasteur's germ theory – that there are **microbes** in the air which cause decay – was an important breakthrough in scientific understanding. It disproved the theory of spontaneous generation and led Koch to identify the specific microbes that caused some individual diseases. As a result of this improved understanding of the causes of diseases, scientists hoped they could find ways of treating them. But this was going to take some time, because they would first need to identify the microbe responsible for each separate disease. Only then could there be a cure.

When Pasteur discovered the technique that created a weakened version of a chicken cholera microbe, almost twenty years later, he realised that vaccines for other diseases could be developed. But this also depended on microbes for each specific disease being identified.

Impact

Despite its importance, this breakthrough in scientific knowledge and understanding had limited impact on medicine at the time because each disease had to be researched individually. Progress in the prevention and treatment of diseases was, therefore, slow.

Activities

1 Explain why Pasteur called his procedure vaccination even though it is a different technique from Jenner's procedure.

2 Why could doctors in the 19th century still not successfully treat illness even after the work of Pasteur and Koch?

3 Why do you think many doctors still recommended regular bloodletting as a preventive measure until the late 19th century?

FASCINATING FACT

As well as bloodletting, purging continued to be used both as a treatment and as a preventive measure. Tobacco vapour or a mixture of water, soap and herbs was used as an enema: it was squirted into the body using a greased pipe.

examzone
Build better answers

What factors led to Pasteur's development of the germ theory? (12 marks)
You may use the following in your answer:
• More powerful microscopes
• Scientific methods
You must also include information of your own.

■ **Basic, Level 1**
Answers make general comments on the germ theory.

 Good, Level 2
Answers describe one of the factors in detail (such as the role of technology leading to more powerful microscopes which meant Pasteur could observe organisms it wasn't possible to see before) or several in little detail.

 Excellent, Level 3
Answers include some explanation of various factors (such as the importance of industry – Pasteur was being financed by the brewing and vinegar industries - and scientific methods of observation and recording) and how these helped Pasteur develop the germ theory. Good use of relevant material and own knowledge to support points.

The importance of research teams

Pasteur and Koch's breakthroughs are good examples of how important research teams were (and are) for scientific research. Pasteur and Koch were both hugely important individuals but they led, and were part of, large teams of researchers who received government funding - they did not work individually.

By the end of the 19th century, scientific research was usually carried out by a team rather than by an individual. A team was more likely to have funding and be able to afford expensive new technology, such as more powerful microscopes. Also, working in a team made it easier to check each other's work and carry out large-scale testing. Furthermore, different members of a team could offer knowledge of different specialisms, for example, medicine, biology and chemistry.

Summary

Pasteur's germ theory was an important breakthrough in understanding disease. It's impact was that it made it possible to develop vaccines to prevent some diseases and eventually led to chemical cures for diseases as we shall see.

3.6 Improvements in medical training

Learning outcomes

By the end of this topic you should be able to:

- explain how doctors' training was improving
- understand the importance of the work of Florence Nightingale in the training of nurses

The influence of John Hunter and others (see pages 40–41) meant that, in 1750–1900, there were more training schools emphasising practical training, examinations and that all doctors needed to be registered.

Doctors' qualifications

In the 18th century, doctors could set up practices once they had been accepted by the Royal College of Surgeons, the Royal College of Physicians or the Society of Apothecaries. Medical training began to improve after 1815 when the Society of Apothecaries and the Royal College of Surgeons introduced examinations before they awarded a certificate. In 1858 the General Medical Act said that a General Medical Council had to be set up and all qualified doctors had to be registered.

However, the fact that doctors could still do relatively little to treat disease meant that they were not always respected.

Practical experience

After Pasteur's germ theory, there was more emphasis on using microscopes and understanding illness, as well as gaining practical experience by observing doctors as they worked in one of the teaching hospitals. Important medical schools developed at Glasgow, Edinburgh, Oxford and London. Once qualified, doctors could apply for a position at a hospital, working under the supervision of an experienced doctor, but they might also volunteer to work at charity hospitals where they would be able to gain more experience. As medical knowledge advanced, doctors tended to divide into general practitioners and those who specialised in specific areas of the body or types of disease – these were usually called consultants.

Source A: A cartoon from 1813 titled 'Giving up the Ghost' showing the prosperous doctor unable to prevent Death at the window coming for his patient.

GIVING UP THE GHOST or ONE TOO MANY.

Dissections

Many medical students recognised the value of dissection and studying the human anatomy personally. As a result, body snatchers operated in the 18th and early 19th centuries, seizing the bodies of hanged criminals or digging up newly buried corpses in order to provide specimens for students. The most famous of these body snatchers were Burke and Hare, who operated in Edinburgh, Scotland. The government tried to end this practice with the Anatomy Act of 1832, which allowed licensed 'anatomists' to take the corpse of anyone dying in the workhouse, who was not claimed by a relative.

The work of Florence Nightingale

If there was no family member to provide care for a sick person, a nurse might be employed. Although proper training for nurses had begun in Germany, at Kaiserwerth in 1833, nursing was still not seen as a respectable career in Britain and therefore most nurses were poor and uneducated.

Florence Nightingale wanted to become a nurse and, despite her wealthy family's objections, she trained at Kaiserwerth hospital in 1850. When she returned to Britain to nurse, she became Superintendent of Nurses in a hospital in London. Due to her family connections with politicians, she was allowed to lead a team of nurses at the military hospital in Scutari during the Crimean War (1854–1856).

The Times publicised the filthy conditions in the Scutari hospital which caused public outrage. Nightingale believed that disease was caused by miasma. She was met with opposition by the doctors at Scutari but organised care and supplies, emphasising cleanliness and fresh air. The death rate fell from 42 to 2 per cent, though the exact cause is unclear. What is clear is that people in Britain believed that Nightingale had had a huge effect.

The significance of Florence Nightingale

Source B: Florence Nightingale (1820–1910).

- Her work in the Crimea was reported in British newspapers and she was greeted as a hero on her return to Britain.

- The public contributed money that helped establish the Nightingale School for Nurses in London in 1860.

- She published *Notes on Nursing* about practical care and high standards – which has been translated into 11 languages.

- She wrote over 200 books about hospital design and organisation.

- She was also influential in establishing a training school for midwives at King's College Hospital, London in 1861.

Activities

1. Explain the changes that happened in the training of doctors between 1750 and 1900.

2. Study Source A. List the points that it is making about doctors at this time.

3. Create an ideas map of the impact of Florence Nightingale. Remember to include her impact on nursing, medical care and hospitals.

 examzone

Build better answers

How important was the work of Florence Nightingale in improving hospital care in the 19th century? Explain your answer.

(16 marks)

You may use the following in your answer:
- The Nightingale School for Nurses
- Pasteur's germ theory

You must also include information of your own.

 Basic, Level 1
Answers offer general statements onNightingale's work.

 Good, Level 2
Answers describe her work in detail.

 Better, Level 3
Answers focus on ways in which she improved hospital care, such as helping to professionalise nursing and improve cleanliness in hospitals, and show some awareness of other factors.

 Excellent, Level 4
Answers weigh up Nightingale's importance by describing and explaining her work and its impact, and that of other factors such as Pasteur's germ theory or public pressure to improve hospital care. Points supported by accurate material.

Make sure you write accurately – there are three extra marks available for spelling, grammar and punctuation in these questions.

Summary

Doctors' training continued to improve between 1750 and 1900. Florence Nightingale helped to professionalise nursing and improve care in hospitals.

3.7 Hospitals and the care of the sick

> ## Learning outcomes
>
> By the end of this topic you should be able to:
>
> - understand the key aspects of improved provision of care for the sick in this period
> - recognise that different social groups received different levels of care
> - analyse the extent of change in the provision of care for the sick

Where were people treated?

In 1859, the first cottage hospital opened in Sussex (by 1900 there were 300 of them). They were usually small and provided nursing care while the medical treatment came from local GPs. At this time there were also 18 voluntary hospitals in London with 4,000 beds. Cottage and voluntary hospitals were funded by individuals or subscription.

Doctors at voluntary hospitals would give their services for free. But by and large where you were treated depended on how much money you had.

- The middle and upper classes, who could afford to pay a doctor's fees, would usually be treated at home.

- Some doctors set up sick clubs, where people could pay a small amount into a fund weekly to cover any costs of treatment from the doctor.

- The working classes could not pay a doctor and might attend the dispensary or out-patients department of a hospital.

- Many old, sick or disabled people who could not support themselves had to enter the local workhouses, which had been set up by the 1834 Poor Law Amendment Act; in the 1860s there were approximately 65,000 people being cared for in this way.

Public concern about care for the poor

In the 1860s there was a lot of publicity about the level of care offered to poor people. The Times newspaper and The Lancet medical journal raised concern about the number of old, sick, blind, deaf or disabled people, or those with mental health issues, who were in workhouses intended to support the unemployed poor. Out of 28,550 places in London, only 3,000 of the people in workhouses were actually able-bodied unemployed. In 1865 Louisa Twining established the Workhouse Visiting Society, which campaigned for workhouse reform and an improved standard of nursing in the workhouse.

Publicity, pressure and change

This public concern joined with the emphasis in new hospital designs on space and ventilation, to put increasing pressure on local public authorities, such as the Poor Law Unions, to improve the provision of hospital care for the poor.

Source A: Mealtime at the St Marylebone's workhouse, 1900: men's dining room.

Source B: The Birmingham New Poor Law infirmary was opened in 1888. Its pavilion plan, on open ground and with separate isolation wards, is the sort of design that Florence Nightingale promoted.

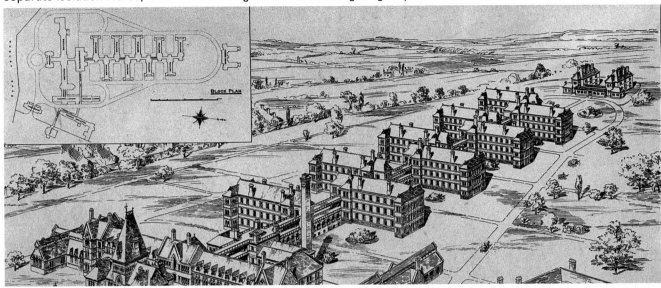

Government action

Starting in London in 1867 but spreading throughout the country, it was ordered that Poor Law Unions should join together to build infirmaries that were separate from the workhouses and that had a fulltime doctor appointed to them. The institutions were paid for by local rate-payers. New asylums for people with mental health issues and fever houses for people with infectious diseases were also built.

These changes were an improvement but didn't completely separate the workhouse and medical treatment for the poor: in 1887 the Birmingham Poor Law Union built a new infirmary with 1,100 beds, but 1,500 old people were still housed in the workhouse three years later. However, by 1900 the Poor Law infirmaries and the fever hospitals and asylums run by local authorities dealt with far more patients than the voluntary hospitals, and these new infirmaries often went on to become major general hospitals with specialist doctors.

Other factors in the development of hospital care

- Nightingale's work in regulating the training of nurses was a significant factor.
- Pasteur's work on germs also had an impact on hospitals. Joseph Lister began to use carbolic acid to create antiseptic conditions during operations. By 1900 most hospitals accepted the need for antiseptic conditions and equipment in the wards.

Activities

1 Why would a government care about what newspapers or medical journals were saying about medical provision for the poor?

2 At the start of this period there was a big difference in the treatment and care received by the rich and that received by the poor. To what extent did this still exist in 1900?

3 How much progress in the treatment of illness and the care of the sick do you think there was during the period 1750–1900?

4 Draw a diagram to summarise the role of the following four factors in the development of hospital care: publicity; government action; developments in nursing care; and medical advances.

Summary

By 1900 there was the recognition that hospital care needed to be improved. The standard of care within workhouses was rising (although there was still great variation between different areas of the country). However, there was no move yet to fund hospitals from central government.

3.8 The trigger for public health action? Cholera, Chadwick and Snow

Learning outcomes

By the end of this topic you should be able to:

- describe the impact of cholera
- understand why it led to an increased search for the cause of disease and improved public health provision
- evaluate the work of Edwin Chadwick and John Snow in improving public health provision

There was already concern about deaths from killer diseases but, in 1831, a new and even more terrifying disease appeared – cholera. Although cholera had been known in India for many centuries, it does not seem to have been present in Britain before this date. It was a frightening disease because people could die within a single day and it spread so quickly that thousands could die within a few weeks.

Source A: The "Silent Highway"-Man. Your money or your life! 1858 Punch cartoon.

THE "SILENT HIGHWAY"-MAN.
"Your MONEY or your LIFE!"

Activities

1 Source A is saying that people should spend money on improving the water quality of the Thames or its impurities will kill them. How is it similar to the Danse Macabre picture relating to the Black Death on page 34?

Treating cholera

The following were all used to prevent and/or treat cholera in the 19th century:

- burning the clothes and bedding of the dead person
- praying
- cleaning the house and scattering chloride of lime around (this was used in whitewash to make things look clean)
- smoking cigars
- lucky charms
- burning barrels of tar or vinegar to create smoke in the streets
- making 'special mixtures' of liquids or pills that were supposed to cure all ills.

Few of these did any good, but the work of two men in particular helped to prevent the spread of cholera and establish what was spreading the disease.

Chadwick's role in improving public health

Local authorities were expected to use taxes to make provision in workhouses for those who were too old, too weak or too ill to support themselves. Edwin Chadwick was secretary to the commission in overall charge of the workhouses. In 1842 Edwin Chadwick published the results of his survey of housing conditions in towns called *Report on the Sanitary Conditions of the Labouring Population of Great Britain*. He suggested it would be cheaper if local taxes (rates) were used to improve housing and hygiene rather than paying for sick people to be supported in the workhouses.

Specific suggestions made by Chadwick were about improvements in providing access to clean water, and the removal of sewage and rubbish. However, Chadwick's suggestions were criticised by some when the report was published.

- At this time there was an attitude of laissez-faire, which was the belief that the government should not interfere in ordinary lives or business.

- The water companies objected to Chadwick's ideas because they thought changes might reduce their profits.
- Middle-class people, who had to pay these local rates, did not see why their money should be taken to provide better living conditions for the poor who did not pay anything towards these improvements.

In 1842 Chadwick's ideas got a lot of attention, but little was actually done. Many people were angry at the idea that the government should insist on piped water and sewers – their complaints led to these protesters being nicknamed the 'Dirty Party'. However, another cholera **epidemic** in 1848 led the government to try out some of Chadwick's ideas (see page 64).

Mapping a connection – Dr John Snow's investigation

In 1854 there was another outbreak of cholera in London, and Dr John Snow used it to investigate the theory that cholera was spread through infected water. He marked on a map all the deaths in one area, and there was a clear concentration of deaths around the water pump on Broad Street. Snow had the handle of that pump removed so that water could not be collected and the number of deaths fell dramatically.

Source B: A section of John Snow's map showing deaths from cholera in 1854 in the Soho area of London

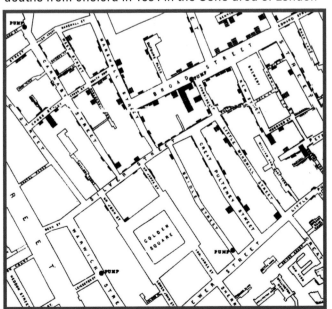

Activities

2   Compare the methods of treatment and prevention of cholera in the 19th century with those of the Great Plague in 1665 (pages 44–45) and the Black Death in 1348 (pages 34–35).

3   How did the following factors prevent Chadwick from being effective: lack of scientific knowledge about disease; limited role of government in public health; and people's attitudes towards health and government action?

4   Explain why John Snow's work would have helped change people's minds about Chadwick's ideas.

examzone

Build better answers

Choose one period and describe the key methods of dealing with epidemics:
- the nineteenth century
- the later Middle Ages.   (6 marks)

■   **Basic, Level 1**
Answers contain limited detail, for example stating that people took medicines or prayed.

●   **Good, Level 2**
Answers describe a range of different methods from individual treatments and prevention methods to attempts by the authorities to improve public health provisions.

Summary

Epidemics of cholera killed thousands but prompted people to try and find solutions to improving public health systems. Chadwick's report highlighted the issues and laid the basis for reform; Snow's work proved the connection between poor water supply and cholera, which added weight to the need for better public health provisions.

3.9 Public health 1750–1900: government action

Learning outcomes

By the end of this topic you should be able to:

- outline the measures of the Public Health Acts of 1848 and 1875
- give reasons why local and national government finally took decisive action
- evaluate the significance of the work done by the authorities in improving public health

The Public Health Act, 1848

In 1848, another serious outbreak of cholera finally prompted the government to take action on Chadwick's ideas. The Public Health Act in 1848 set up a General Board of Health, with Chadwick as one of the three commissioners. It also allowed towns to:

- set up their own local Board of Health
- appoint a local medical officer
- organise the removal of rubbish
- build a sewer system.

But it did not force town councils to do this, unless the local death rate passed 23 per thousand living. Only one-third of towns set up a Board of Health and even fewer appointed a medical officer. Meanwhile, the terms of the Act were only temporary so that, in 1854, the three commissioners had to resign and the General Board of Health was abolished in 1858. Chadwick was not appointed to any other official position.

What prompted further action?

Parliament slowly became convinced during the 1850s and 1860s that it should take further action to improve public health and that these measures should be compulsory.

- Snow's work (1854) seemed to prove there was a link between water and cholera.
- Pasteur's germ theory showed how disease spread and why hygiene was important.
- Snow also showed that death rates varied according to the water sources used by different water companies.
- The government started collecting statistics on births, marriages and deaths; William Farr studied these and showed that the death rates were much higher in the towns and cities than in villages.

Local councils take action

Another outbreak of cholera in 1866 least affected those towns where there had already been some improvements in public health. This reinforced the link between hygiene and health. When working-class men living in towns got the vote in 1867, they used their voice to put even more pressure on the government and on local councils to take action. A good example of this is that, in the 1870s, Joseph Chamberlain, the mayor of Birmingham, carried out several reforms, including the demolition of 40 acres of slums.

A COURT FOR KING CHOLERA.

Source A: A cartoon called 'A Court for King Cholera' published in 1852. It shows that people at the time understood that cholera was likely to spread in dirty and overcrowded conditions.

The Public Health Act, 1875

Parliament began passing more legislation on public health.

- The 1866 Sanitary Act forced all towns to appoint inspectors to check water supplies and drainage.
- The 1875 Artisans Dwelling Act gave local authorities the power to buy and demolish slum housing.
- These led to the 1875 Public Health Act - which made local councils responsible for ensuring that the following were provided:

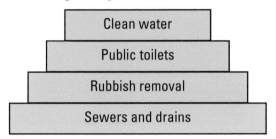

Clean water

Public toilets

Rubbish removal

Sewers and drains

The Act also made towns appoint Health and Sanitary Inspectors and a Medical Officer of Health.

In the years after 1875, local councils also became responsible for:

- checking the quality of food in shops
- ensuring that the quality of new housing was improved
- enforcing a new law against polluting water supplies such as rivers and streams.

Despite this, in many towns, basic services such as water, lighting and paving were still in the hands of private companies and individuals.

Compulsory vaccinations

Another way in which the government became more involved in healthcare was through compulsory vaccinations. When Jenner discovered a way of preventing people catching smallpox, the role of the government was crucial (see pages 54–55). Although the Jennerian society was set up to offer free vaccinations, many people still distrusted the idea of using cowpox to vaccinate against smallpox. The government made vaccination compulsory in 1852, but it was not strictly enforced until 1871 when an Act of Parliament forced local authorities to register everyone who was vaccinated – only then did the number of deaths from smallpox drop dramatically.

As scientists developed other vaccines for killer diseases, the government campaigned for people to start vaccinating their children and then made some vaccines compulsory. This, arguably, was as important as developing the vaccines themselves in reducing deaths from these diseases.

Source B: Graph showing deaths from killer diseases, when microbes were identified, when vaccines were developed and when there was a government campaign for vaccination.

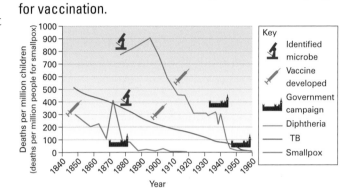

Activities

1 Chadwick did not properly understand the link between health and hygiene, and the reforms based on his ideas were all temporary. Does that mean Chadwick was a failure?

2 The reforms of 1875 went much further than the reforms of 1848. Why were they accepted when there had been so much opposition to the earlier ideas?

3 Study Source B. Explain how the graph shows the importance of the following factors in preventing disease at the end of the 19th century:

   a) improvements in scientific knowledge

   b) the role of the government.

4 Why do you think the death rate for TB (indicated by the blue line on the graph) was falling even before the vaccine was developed?

Summary

In the second half of the 19th century there was greater acceptance of the need for action by central government and local authorities to improve public health. Change was rapid and far-reaching.

3.10 Public health 1750–1900: the role of technology

The 'Great Stink' 1858

Plans were already being made for a new sewer system in London in 1858. However, the extremely hot weather meant that the level of the River Thames was low and the smell of the exposed sewage along its banks was so great that parliament could not meet, even though sheets soaked in disinfectant were hung at the windows to cover up the smell. This 'Great Stink' combined with outbreaks of cholera, and the work of people such as Chadwick and Snow, to convince the authorities that more public health reform was needed.

Joseph Bazalgette

The Metropolitan Board of Works agreed to the expensive ideas being put forward by Joseph Bazalgette for a new sewer system in London. Bazalgette was an engineer who had worked in the railway industry before working on large-scale sewage and drainage projects. He designed a complex sewerage system for London that took into consideration future population growth as well as the needs of the time. It included 1,300 miles of sewers, plus pumping stations and embankments besides the River Thames to house the stations. It took Bazalgette and his huge team of engineers and construction workers over seven years to complete.

> **FASCINATING FACT**
>
> Queen Victoria was so excited about the new large sewer tunnels that she ordered a small railway line to be installed to transport people through the sewer. Gas lights and walkways were installed, with booths selling souvenirs.

Source A: A photograph of Bazalgette inspecting the construction of the London sewer system.

Source B: An illustration showing the planning and engineering work involved in the construction of London's underground sewer system.

The role of industry and technology

Sources A and B show the size of the sewers created, the construction work they required and the complexity of planning and engineering that went into London's new underground sewer system. This highlights another important factor in improving public heath – technology and industry.

Although the industrial revolution led to many public health problems, it also provided some of the solutions. Through designing and building machinery for farms and factories, and the development of the railway and canal systems, people had learned the best ways of building pipelines, tunnels and embankments and how to harness the power of steam to run engines.

The pumping station shown in Source C was installed in 1865 in London. The engine shown was one of four engines used to pump water through London's sewers. They worked tirelessly until they were replaced by a more modern system in the 1950s! Machines and systems such as this would have been impossible to achieve before the technological developments of the industrial revolution.

Source C: This pumping station was part of Bazalgette's new sewer system.

Activities

1 Research: find out more about the work of Joseph Bazalgette. Then write a newspaper article, set in 1866, arguing either that his work on London's sewer system has been a great advance in public health or a huge waste of money.

2 List as many examples of 19th century technology as you can think of. Then think of ways in which this technology has been used for public health systems.

3 You have now looked at the role of science (e.g. Pasteur), the role of government action (e.g. the Public Health Act of 1875) and the role of industry and technology (e.g. the planning and construction of Bazalgette's sewer system). Which of these do you think was the most important in improving public health provision?

4 Evaluate the impact of cholera on public health provision. Do you think any of the public health improvements would have been made without the continuing outbreaks of this disease? Explain your answer.

 examzone **Watch out!**

Remember that no single factor was totally responsible for public health improvements. They all relied upon each other. For example, the government action in making proper sewers in towns compulsory would not have been so effective if the technology and knowledge of how to create these sewers didn't exist!

Summary

Industry and technology played a role in improving public health systems in towns and cities. Key individuals, such as Joseph Bazalgette, were important in accelerating change or steering its direction.

3.11 Change and continuity: how much did medicine and public health change between 1750 and 1900?

Learning outcomes

By the end of this topic you should be able to:

- assess the significance of key individuals in the development of medical knowledge
- identify the role of different factors affecting developments in medicine and public health
- understand how attitudes are often slow to change

The importance of individuals

1 Copy and complete the chart below, comparing the importance of key individuals in this period.
2 Who was the most important of these individuals in bringing about advances in medicine in this period? Explain your answer.
3 How far do you think Pasteur's germ theory can be described as a turning point in medicine?
4 Pasteur and Koch worked in research teams, which played a vital role in carrying out their experiments. Explain how and why working in teams of researchers was more effective than working individually.
5 Explain why the advances in medicine that were made during the period 1750–1900 could not have been made during the Middle Ages or the Renaissance period.

	Jenner	Pasteur	Koch
What did they do?			
What effect did it have on medicine or treatment at the time?			
What was the long term effect of their work?			
What factors were involved?			

Review

6 Look back to pages 46–47. In the activities you were asked to sort key points into two lists, showing points leading to progress and points that held back developments in medicine.

Use those ideas to do your own review of medicine in the period 1750–1900.

Changes in hospitals

The Great Ormond Street Hospital for sick children was opened in 1852 and contained only ten beds. Source A – from 1856 – shows how the first ward tried to recreate a home atmosphere, but by the time of the new ward in Source B – built in 1875 – the emphasis was on medicine as a science and a professional approach to the design of hospital wards and to nursing care.

7 Explain how the changes shown in the pictures of the ward in Great Ormond Street Hospital reflect the changing approaches to medicine in the period 1750–1900.
8 What factors do you think were important in influencing these changes?

Source A: Great Ormond Street Hospital in 1856.

Resistance to change

There was often resistance to change from doctors, government and the general public. For example, there was resistance to Jenner's vaccination against smallpox, both within the medical profession and from the public. For this reason, advances in medicine were sometimes slow to make an impact. However, the role of newspapers and the development of photographs meant that people became more aware of problems, and public pressure sometimes forced change to happen more quickly. You can see this in the concern about the poor in the late-19th century and the moves to improve care of the sick.

9 Look at the points below. Give examples from the period 1750–1900 to show how each of these could be a factor holding back change, helping to promote change, or both!

a) communication and publicity of new ideas
b) education and training of medical professionals
c) government action (or lack of it)
d) industrialisation
e) general attitudes to new ideas
f) religious or social beliefs
g) science
h) technology

Source B: Great Ormond Street Hospital in 1875.

Wooden floors for easy cleaning

Tidy and orderly appearance

Clean sheets

Big windows for light and ventilation

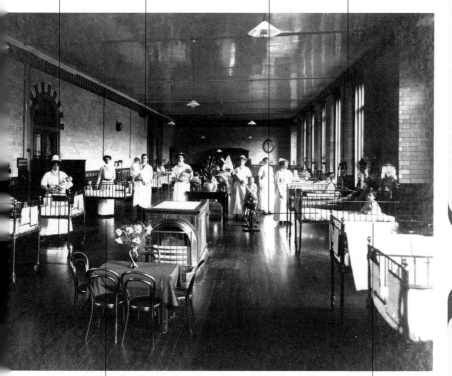

Nurses have a central role on the ward; they are in uniforms, including caps

Parents and visitors are not required to help with patient care and visiting is now restricted

Build better answers

What do Sources A and B show about the changes made in hospitals in the 19th century? Explain your answer, using Sources A and B and your own knowledge. (8 marks)

■ **Basic, Level 1**
Answers mention general comments on hospital changes.

● **Good, Level 2**
Answers state changes shown in the sources and/or use their own knowledge to place these changes into historical context.

▲ **Excellent, Level 3**
Answers comment on the nature or extent of change based on the content of the sources, supported with their own knowledge.

Summary

There were some significant developments in medicine between 1750 and 1900, especially in understanding the causes of disease, but there were also many elements of continuity, for example, few poor people had access to doctors or medical care.

3.12 Historians' use of statistics

70

Learning outcome

By the end of this topic you should be able to:

- understand how to interpret and evaluate statistical sources

It is tempting to think that statistics are totally reliable, especially when the figures look very precise. However, historians must treat them in the same way as they use all sources and ask the following questions.

1 Who produced the source?

2 Why did they produce the source?

3 Where did they get their information from?

4 Can it be assumed that any information and conclusions based on these figures also applies to other areas in the country?

In 1665, when there was an epidemic of the plague in London, women were employed as searchers to record the number of the dead. If someone had died from the plague, their whole family was locked into the house for 28 days to prevent them spreading the plague any further.

Source A: Bill of mortality for the week beginning 15 August 1665.

Abortive 5
Aged 43
Ague 2
Apoplexie 1
Bleeding 2
Burnt in his bed by a candle at St Giles Cripplegate 1
Canker 1
Childbed 42
Chrisomes 18
Consumption 134
Convulsion 64
Cough 2
Dropsie 33
Feaver 309
Flox and smallpox 5

Frighted 3
Gowt 1
Grief 3
Griping in the guts 51
Jaundies 5
Imposthume 11
Infants 16
Killed by a fall from the Belfry at Allhallows the Great 1
Kingsevil 2
Lethargy 1
Palsie 1
Plague 7165
Rickets 17
Rising of the Lights 11
Scowring 5

Scurvy 2
Spleen 1
Spotted Feaver 101
Stillborn 17
Stone 2
Stopping of the stomach 9
Strangury 1
Suddenly 1
Surfeit 49
Teeth 121
Thrush 5
Timpany 1
Tissick 11
Vomiting 3
Winde 3
Wormes 15

Christened { Males 95 / Females 81 / In all 176 }

Buried { Males 4095 / Females 4202 / In all 8297 } Plague 7165

Increased in the Burials this Week 607

Parishes clear of the Plague 4

Parishes Infected 126

Activities

1 Find three examples of diseases listed in Source A that could also have been the plague.

2 Why might the searcher not have listed the cause of death accurately even if it really was caused by the plague?

3 Find at least one other example of something listed as a cause of death, which you feel is not accurate. Can you think why it has been recorded that way?

4 Samuel Pepys lived in London and kept a diary of his experiences during the 1660s. He wrote on 30 August 1665 that the parish clerk had said that, out of every nine people who died of the plague, he only recorded six plague deaths. Using this information and Source A, what do you think the accurate total of plague deaths could have been for this week in August?

5 Pepys also said that the poor died in such numbers that they were not always recorded. Does that mean that Source A is of no use to historians? Explain your answer.

Before the 19th century, population details were not very accurate. Most priests kept records of births and deaths but this information was not sent to any central government office. Many of these records have not survived because the papers have been damaged or simply lost. However:

- In 1801 the government ordered every parish to send in details about the number of houses and the number of families in their area, the number of christenings, marriages and burials, and whether people were employed. This is a census.
- In 1821 the census added people's age.
- In 1841 the census also added gender and occupation.

Other useful information comes from local authorities who began to employ Medical Health Officers who sent annual statistics to central government. You can see from the table that the information tells us the age of death for each person, their gender and what they died from.

Activities

6 Why might you expect the figures given in Source B to be more accurate than the figures in Source A?

7 Why might the figures in Source B still not be totally accurate?

8 Even if Source B is mainly accurate, it does not give us the full picture. For example, a patient might be weakened so much by an illness that they then die from something like bronchitis and pneumonia.

a) Think of three questions you would like to ask about Source B.

b) Explain what other sources of information you would need to consult in order to find out your answers.

9 What different types of sources would you use if you were going to research the history of your local hospital? For each source explain why it would be useful and what limitations it could have.

Source B: The table shows deaths in Maidstone in 1889.

TABLE OF DEATHS during the year 1889, in the Urban Sanitary District of Maidstone																		
		DEATHS FROM ALL CAUSES							DEATHS FROM SPECIFIED CAUSES									
	Estimated to middle 1889	At all ages	Under 5	5 and under 15	15 and under 25	25 and under 60	60 and upwards		Smallpox	Measles	Diphtheria	Typhoid	Diarrhoea and Dysentery	Cholera	Bronchitis, Pneumonia and Pleurisy	Heart disease	Injuries	All other diseases
EAST MAIDSTONE Males	15,422	113	47	9	3	26	28	Under 5		6	2		4		5		4	26
								5 upwards		1					13	6	4	42
Females		120	52	8	4	15	41	Under 5		9	1		3		7	2	2	28
								5 upwards	1	2					9	9	2	45
Total		233																
WEST MAIDSTONE Males	14,201	107	50	5	10	19	23	Under 5		4	5		3		7	1		30
								5 upwards		5					6	4	10	32
Females		110	41	13	4	21	31	Under 5		1	6		1		6		1	26
								5 upwards		7	1	1			15	8		37
Total		217																
Totals	29,623	450	190	35	21	81	123	Under 5		20	14		11		25	3	7	110
								5 upwards	1	15	1	1			43	27	16	156

4.1 Medicine and public health c1900 to present day: introduction

This section begins with a quick overview of the enormous changes that happened in the 20th century before examining these changes and the reasons for them in more detail. As you study this, you should focus on the key themes about the process of change in medicine and public health. Those key themes are:

- ideas about the cause and treatment of disease and illness
- approaches to public health and prevention of disease and illness
- the influence of changes in society on medicine and public health.

Before...

The rapid industrial changes in the 19th century caused a new set of health problems, but science and technology also helped to create a better understanding of disease and provided some ways to prevent disease spreading. The government became more involved in dealing with health and disease but the standards of health care still tended to depend upon people's ability to pay.

After...

As the cost of the NHS (National Health Service) continues to rise, there is great debate about the role of government and private health schemes in health care provision. Developments in science and technology have raised hopes of cures for many diseases and conditions but have also led to a debate about ethics within medicine, especially in genetic and embryo research.

exam zone

Watch out!

Many students assume that modern medicine is a story of continual progress but this is not always the case. You will study an example of this on pages 90–91.

Antibiotics: Drugs that stop infections caused by bacteria

Consultant: A doctor specialising in a specific disease or part of the body; usually based in hospital

Crystallography: Using radiation to take a high-power X-ray photograph

DNA: The abbreviation for deoxyribonucleic acid, which contains the genetic instructions for every cell in your body

General practitioner (GP): A doctor who works in a practice dealing directly with the public

Genetics: The study of genes and inherited characteristics

Immunisation: the process of making someone immune to a disease, including inoculation and vaccination

Magic bullet: A chemical drug that kills the microbes causing a specific disease without harming the rest of the body

National Health Service (NHS): An organisation set up by the government in 1948 to give free health care to all

Pharmaceutical industry: The business of manufacturing medicinal drugs prescribed by a doctor or sold by a chemist

Pharmacy: A business selling medical drugs; a chemist's shop

Prescription charges: Payment for medicine prescribed by a doctor

Radiotherapy: The use of radiation in medicine, often to attack cancer

Welfare state: The coordination and provision by the government of all matters affecting the health of the people

---

1911
National Insurance introduced

1919
Nursing Act

1941
Mass production of penicillin began

1948
The establishment of the NHS in Britain

1953
Watson and Crick show the structure of DNA

2003
Human Genome Project completed

2007
Smoking in public places banned in England and Wales

4.2 Why did life expectancy increase in the 20th century?

Learning outcome

By the end of this topic you should be able to:

- Understand some of the reasons why life expectancy increased during the 20th century

At the start of the 20th century, photographs, film, electricity, the bicycle and the motor car had all been invented but many people continued to live and work in cramped and unhygienic conditions, using oil lamps or gas lighting. Despite medical advances, many people would simply not be able to afford to see a doctor and the average life expectancy in 1901 was only 47. Pasteur's germ theory had led to a range of vaccinations being developed but there had been little progress in the search for a way to cure diseases and most medicines were still based on mixtures of ingredients such as plants and spices.

The 20th century was a story of huge improvements in the treatment of illness. Most people in the UK now have better living standards than in the 19th century, and often better diets as a result of our increased prosperity.

We also tend to assume that, even if we don't have a cure for an illness now, science will probably find one in the future, and we can successfully treat far more health problems, such as heart conditions.

Activities

A drawing showing the living conditions of families in slum housing in the early 1900s.

1 What clues are there in the above picture to suggest that there was a low standard of living among the poor at the start of the 20th century?

2 The two charts on this page are comparing the main causes of death in 1900 with the main causes of death in 1997.

   a) What were the three main causes of death in 1900?

   b) What were the three main causes of death in 1997?

   c) Why do you think the main causes of death changed during the 20th century?

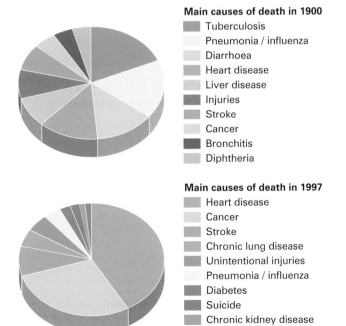

Main causes of death in 1900
- Tuberculosis
- Pneumonia / influenza
- Diarrhoea
- Heart disease
- Liver disease
- Injuries
- Stroke
- Cancer
- Bronchitis
- Diphtheria

Main causes of death in 1997
- Heart disease
- Cancer
- Stroke
- Chronic lung disease
- Unintentional injuries
- Pneumonia / influenza
- Diabetes
- Suicide
- Chronic kidney disease
- Chronic liver disease

Summary

- In 1900 poor standards of living and a limited ability to treat illness meant that life expectancy was still low.

- The 20th century saw great improvements, which had a major effect on life expectancy, increasing it from 47 to 79 by 2001.

4.3 Developments in the fight against disease

Learning outcomes

By the end of this topic you should be able to:

- understand the development of vaccinations
- understand the factors involved in the development of magic bullets to cure disease
- evaluate the significance of the development of magic bullets in finding cures for diseases

Cause and prevention of disease

Earlier (pages 56–57), you saw how Pasteur's germ theory was an important breakthrough in understanding the causes of many diseases and how the work of Pasteur and Koch led to the development of vaccinations to prevent disease.

You can see the results of this breakthrough in the table of vaccinations below.

Pasteur's germ theory in 1861 was an important breakthrough in understanding how disease is spread.

↓

It led to Koch's work in identifying the different microbes that cause disease.

↓

The technique to prevent people from catching a disease was developed and applied to more and more diseases.

↓

The government also began to intervene more in people's lives. They first encouraged and then later insisted that all children were vaccinated.

Vaccination timeline

1896	Typhoid	1950s	Polio
1906	Tuberculosis	1964	Measles
1913	Diphtheria	1988	MMR (Measles, Mumps, Rubella)
1927	Tetanus		
1952	Whooping cough	2008	Cervical cancer

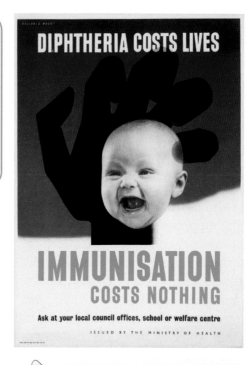

Source A: A poster advertising immunisation.

examzone **Watch out!**

Remember – vaccinations *prevent* disease, they do not *cure* them!

Activities

1 As you read the text on the next page, copy and complete the flow chart below to show the different stages in the development of magic bullets.

Behring's work showed that …

↓

Ehrlich's research showed that …

↓

Hata showed that …

↓

Magic bullets were an important medical breakthrough because…

The first magic bullet

Improved understanding of the causes of disease also led to a search for 'magic bullets' that would cure diseases.

- Emil von Behring developed Koch's work to isolate the antitoxins used by the body to fight diphtheria – then found a way to inject them to cure the disease.
- Paul Ehrlich (a member of Koch's team) now set up his own research team to build on this work. Ehrlich knew certain dyes stained specific microbes (Koch's work) and antitoxins only attacked the disease microbes (Behring's work).
- Ehrlich tried to combine a dye with other chemicals to find a cure for syphilis – a 'magic bullet' that would only target the disease microbe and not harm the rest of the body.
- Ehrlich researched for several years (this was only possible because he received German government funds).
- In 1909 Dr Sahachiro Hata joined the team from Japan and reviewed some previous experiments. He discovered a mistake – the 606th compound that they had tested and dismissed was actually effective! This treatment was called Salvarsan 606.

The second magic bullet

The use of chemical drugs to target and cure illness was an important breakthrough. However, it was not until 1932 that a second magic bullet was found, when Gerhard Domagk discovered that a particular red dye was effective against some cases of blood poisoning and he developed the drug Prontosil. Many people died after simple cuts or scratches became infected, so this cure for blood poisoning could save many lives.

FASCINATING FACT

Domagk's daughter pricked her finger on a needle and was dying from blood poisoning. He had not tested Prontosil on humans, only on mice, but he risked using it – and saved her life.

Research showed that the key ingredient which made Prontosil effective was the sulphonamide (a chemical compound). This led to the development of other drugs based on different sulphonamides that could cure pneumonia, scarlet fever and meningitis.

These discoveries were important because medicine could now cure many of the infections and diseases that had previously led to death. At first, treatment tended to be by injection, but the developments in technology in the late 19th century had made it possible to mass-produce pills and now the **pharmaceutical industry** began to grow rapidly.

Activities

2 Use the information in this section to explain how the science of chemistry helped in the development of medical cures.

3 Draw an ideas map to show the different factors affecting the discovery of magic bullets.

4 Explain how the discovery of magic bullets can be seen as a turning point for medicine in the 20th century.

Challenge

5 Design a page about magic bullets for a website on the history of medicine. Your website page should include each of the following:
- a timeline
- a picture of a famous person involved in the development of magic bullets
- an explanation of each stage in the work
- an explanation of why this work was important
- a diagram to support some of your comments
- links to other website pages.

exam zone **Watch out!**

Remember – vaccinations prevent disease, they do not cure them!

Summary

Scientific research led to a better understanding of the individual microbes that cause disease. This led to more vaccinations as well as the discovery of 'magic bullets' (a way of using chemicals to target and kill specific microbes), which created the first synthetic cure for many diseases.

4.4 The development of antibiotics

Learning outcomes

By the end of this topic you should be able to:

- describe the work of Fleming and of Florey and Chain in the discovery of penicillin
- understand the factors involved in the discovery of penicillin
- evaluate the roles played by Fleming and by Florey and Chain in the discovery of penicillin

FASCINATING FACT

Fleming did not actually make a new discovery – there are records from the Middle Ages, and even earlier, of people using mouldy bread to fight infection even though they didn't understand why. There is also a record of a doctor called Joseph Lister (see page 118) using penicillin to fight infection in a patient in 1871.

Alexander Fleming was a chemist working at St Mary's Hospital in London. In 1928 he noticed that a culture of bacteria growing in a Petri dish was being attacked and killed by an unknown mould growing in the same dish.

This ruined his experiment but he decided to research the mystery killer mould before throwing it away. He discovered that it was an excellent antibiotic, penicillin, but he only tested it on bacteria in the laboratory, not on bacteria in living organisms.

Fleming published his findings in 1929 but he was unable to get funding to develop his work so he returned to his original research.

It was difficult to produce pure penicillin and so it did not seem practical to try to use it in medicine. However, Howard Florey and Ernst Chain, two scientists working in Oxford, read about Fleming's research and in 1939 they set up a research team, including a range of specialists, to develop penicillin.

In 1940 they tested it on mice, and in 1941 they conducted tests on a patient. The test showed that penicillin acted like a miracle drug on people who were dying from infection. Unfortunately, there was only a small amount of penicillin available and the patient died when the penicillin ran out.

Florey became determined to develop the mass production of penicillin but it could not be synthesised from chemicals (like Salvarsan 606 or Prontosil). The mould had to be cultured on a broth and exposed to air in order to grow. This meant that they had to use a collection of containers, including baths, bedpans, milk churns and food tins, and had to hire six assistants just to deal with this stage of the work. No British firm was able to create the technology needed to mass produce penicillin – partly because many factories were being damaged by the bombing raids during the Second World War or were already working to full capacity producing other drugs needed during the war.

Florey refused to patent penicillin, believing it should be available for everyone, and in June 1941 Florey and Norman Heatley (another member of the team) went to the USA to see if pharmaceutical companies there would fund their research.

At first they were unsuccessful but in December 1941 the USA entered the Second World War and the US government was now prepared to fund the mass production of penicillin. They knew that in war many soldiers were likely to die from infection rather than from actual injuries and so mass-produced penicillin could save many lives. This injection of money allowed the pharmaceutical companies to invest in large-scale production.

Florey had discovered that drying the mould at low temperatures was the most successful method of purifying penicillin. Scientists at the chemical company Pfizer, in New York, used an old ice-cream freezer to develop a method of freeze-drying that was eventually used for large-scale production in 1944.

FASCINATING FACT

In their early tests to discover the best medium to use for producing penicillin, Florey and Chain used Marmite. Later tests found that mouldy cantaloupe melons produced the most penicillin mould.

examzone

Build better answers

Why was the Second World War an important factor in the development of penicillin as a mass vaccine? (12 marks)

You may use the following in your answer.
- Alexander Fleming
- Florey and Chain

You must also include information of your own.

■ **Basic, Level 1**
Answers make general comments about the production of penicillin.

● **Good, Level 2**
Answers describe the work of Fleming and/ or Florey and Chain and other factors in the development of penicillin. Will often include factors from own knowledge, e.g. funds from government.

▲ **Excellent, Level 3**
Answers explain the factors that prevented Fleming and delayed Florey and Chain in mass producing penicillin and explain how these factors were overcome. Also includes factors from own knowledge, e.g. the role of government or war.

Activities

1 Create a timeline for the discovery and mass production of penicillin 1871–1944. On your timeline, colour code the work of:

a) Fleming and

b) Florey and Chain.

2 How fair do you think it was that, when a Nobel Prize was awarded for the discovery of penicillin, it was given jointly to the three men, Fleming, Florey and Chain? Explain your answer.

3 Complete the following diagram showing the role of factors in the development of penicillin.

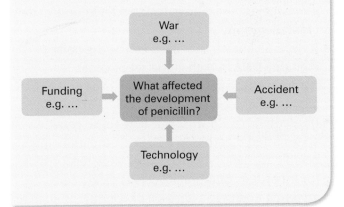

Summary

The development of an antibiotic that could cure bacterial disease and infection was a major advance in medicine. The use of natural organisms to fight bacteria was effective in many cases where chemical drugs were not and, once penicillin was mass produced, it could save thousands of lives.

4.5 The discovery of the double helix and the genetic revolution

78

Learning outcomes

- describe how the discovery of DNA has helped scientists to understand the causes of more diseases
- evaluate the significance of the discovery of the DNA structure in creating the potential for future medical treatment
- understand the relative importance of the factors involved in the discovery of DNA and its future potential in medical treatment

Source A: The double helix structure of DNA.

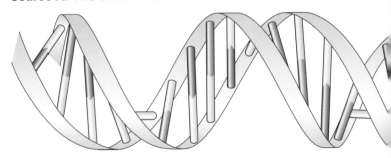

DNA opens the door to new cures for genetic conditions!

1953 Crick and Watson discovered the structure of DNA.

1990 The Human Genome Project, led by Watson, set out to map the location of every single one of the 30,000–35,000 genes in the 23 chromosomes in every cell of the human body.

The project involved hundreds of scientists working in 18 teams. The first draft was produced in 2000.

Scientists have identified certain genes that pass on specific hereditary conditions.

Background

- Study of **genetics** began in the 19th century, when Mendel showed how characteristics can be passed down from one generation to the next.
- During the 20th century, scientists could take photographs of human cells through two improvements in technology – electron microscopes and X-rays (using a technique called **crystallography**).
- It became known that each cell in the body contains **DNA**, which is the set of codes controlling the genes that decide eyes and hair colour, height, and so on.
- If scientists could work out how these genetic codes fitted together in a DNA strand, they might be able to identify which genes were responsible for inherited conditions (such as sickle cell anaemia and cystic fibrosis) or conditions such as Down's syndrome.

Francis Crick and James Watson, two Cambridge scientists, worked together to investigate the structure of DNA. Crick was a physicist and Watson a chemist, but their work also made use of X-ray crystallography by Maurice Wilkins and Rosalind Franklin at King's College Hospital in London. In fact, it was one of Franklin's photographs that suggested that genes were arranged in a double helix structure.

There are new techniques for skin grafts, better production of insulin for diabetics, and better vaccines.

There is a better understanding of conditions such as Down's syndrome and leukaemia, and whether people are more likely to develop certain forms of cancer.

The result

There has been further research to develop techniques to alter faulty genes within the body and prevent genetic illnesses from developing.

The discovery has been made that stem cells (found in the bone marrow of long bones and the pelvis) can transform into various types of cells used around the body – which offers a chance of replacing faulty cells with healthy ones.

Research into genetic conditions requires very specialised knowledge and expensive, high-tech equipment, but it offers exciting possibilities. The diagram shows some of the areas of current research.

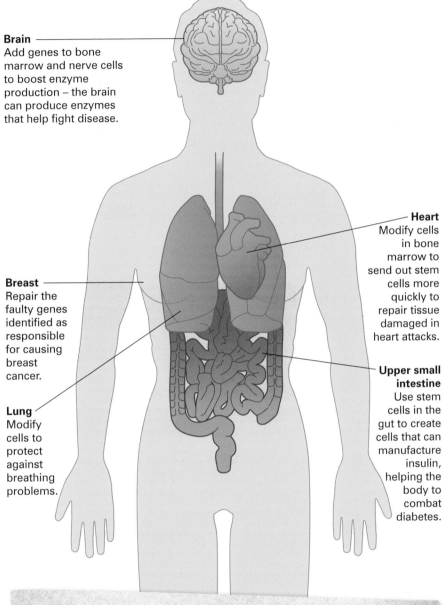

Brain
Add genes to bone marrow and nerve cells to boost enzyme production – the brain can produce enzymes that help fight disease.

Breast
Repair the faulty genes identified as responsible for causing breast cancer.

Lung
Modify cells to protect against breathing problems.

Heart
Modify cells in bone marrow to send out stem cells more quickly to repair tissue damaged in heart attacks.

Upper small intestine
Use stem cells in the gut to create cells that can manufacture insulin, helping the body to combat diabetes.

FASCINATING FACT

The order of the genes within the DNA strand is unique for every single human, except identical twins. For this reason, DNA testing is used to establish the relationship between people, and can be used by the police to identify individuals.

Activities

1 Explain the roles played by science, technology and communication in the discovery of DNA structure.

2 Research – find out about recent developments in genetic medical research, for example embryo research, genetic screening, or the attempts to 'fix' faulty genes.

3 How do you think students in a hundred years will view these early stages of genetic treatment?

• As a turning point where humans discovered the secret to end all disease?

• As an important stage in the development of medicine (like the germ theory)?

Or is there a chance that it will not lead to new discoveries (like Jenner's vaccinations)?

Summary

The discovery of the structure of DNA by Crick and Watson made use of a wide range of specialist knowledge. Further research improved our understanding of genetic conditions and now scientists are beginning to use that knowledge in order to treat and prevent those conditions.

4.6 The role of science and technology in 20th century medicine

Learning outcomes

By the end of this topic you should be able to:

- give examples of ways that science and technology have contributed to medical advances in the 20th century
- evaluate the role played by science and technology within medicine in the 20th century

Science

In the 20th century, scientific research and knowledge has led to:

- chemical treatment of disease (magic bullets)
- **antibiotics**, which used living organisms to fight disease
- more vaccines to prevent the spread of disease
- a better understanding of genetics: genetic changes that cause problems and genetic changes that can help
- treatments being developed for conditions, such as diabetes, which were previously incurable.

Blood transfusions

In the past, most attempts at transfusions had led to the death of the patient, but in 1901 Karl Landsteiner discovered that there were four different blood groups, and transfusions were only successful if the donor's and patient's blood groups were the same.

This discovery meant that:

- people who might die from losing a lot of blood could now be kept alive
- people with blood disorders (such as anaemia) could receive treatment.

The only problem was that blood could not be stored (it clotted), so the donor and the patient had to be together, for the transfusion to be carried out. The high number of injuries during the First World War (1914–1918) sped up the search for a solution.

In 1915, it was discovered that adding sodium citrate prevented blood from clotting, but the blood cells soon deteriorated. In 1916, new scientific techniques made it possible to store blood for longer periods. This made it possible to establish blood banks.

Source A: Different blood groups stored ready for transfusion.

Activities

1 Technology has played an increasingly important role in medicine since 1900 in three main ways. For each of the examples on the next page, decide whether they:
   - support medical research in understanding disease
   - help diagnose and/or monitor a condition
   - treat illness.

2 Of the three ways mentioned in Activity 1, which do you think is the most important aspect of technology as it affects medicine?

3 Overall, how much do you think science has helped medicine to progress since 1900?

X-ray machines

X-rays were discovered by the scientist Wilhelm Roentgen in 1895. The first x-ray machines were developed and were used to diagnose broken bones and some diseases. They began to be used extensively during the First World War.

Radiotherapy and chemotherapy

By 1902, scientists had used Roentgen's discovery to make another one – x-rays could be used to 'burn' and shrink tumours. This led to techniques called **radiotherapy** and chemotherapy which are used today to treat many types of cancer.

X-ray crystallography

This was developed in the first half of the 20th century and enabled scientists to take powerful images of human cells. (Remember that this played a role in the discovery of the structure of DNA.)

Source B: Incubators help keep premature babies alive.

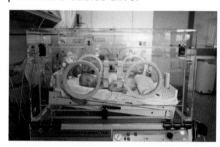

Microscopes

The powerful electron microscope was invented in 1931. It was, and still is, used in medical research and in diagnosis.

Endoscope

This is a flexible tube containing a camera which can be passed inside the body so doctors can see what is happening without the need for surgery.

Scans

X-ray machines were only the first of many types of scanning machines (for example, ultrasound and MRI) which are used to scan a patient and diagnose internal problems.

Medical technology in the 20th and 21st centuries

Source C: An MRI scan showing a brain tumour.

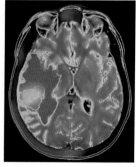

Nuclear medicine

Radioactive elements can be injected into the bloodstream to help track and diagnose what is happening inside the body.

Pacemakers

These are used to help people's hearts work properly.

Dialysis machines

These keep people alive when their kidneys are not functioning properly.

Dispensing instruments

Hypodermic needles and intravenous drips help to give a precise dose of medicine.

FASCINATING FACT

Ultrasound scans, used to study the unborn baby in the womb, are based on sonar technology originally used by submarines.

Summary

Advances in scientific knowledge have had a huge impact on medical research, diagnosis and treatment in the 20th century but they rely on developments in technology. Both science and technology have helped numerous people with medical conditions that would have previously killed them.

4.7 Care of the sick c1900–1948

Learning outcomes

By the end of this topic you should be able to:

- understand the extent of the improvement in medical care during the early 20th century
- understand the key factors affecting these improvements

The early 20th century

At the start of the 20th century, it was still the women in the family who were mainly responsible for treating most illnesses and caring for the sick. Because doctors had to be paid for every visit, people would only use doctors if they were really ill, so most illnesses were treated with preparations bought from a chemist. Traditional 'folk remedies' continued to be used, such as a red cloth to help you recover from a cold or influenza and a sweaty sock tied around the neck to help a sore throat. Minor surgery, such as taking out tonsils, was often done by a doctor on the kitchen table. A **general practitioner** (GP) might also do some minor surgery in a local cottage hospital but anything serious would be referred to a specialist consultant in a big hospital.

examzone

Build better answers

How useful is this photograph to a historian who is investigating access to healthcare in the first half of the 20th century? Use Source B and your own knowledge to explain your answer. (8 marks)

■ **Basic, Level 1**
Answers assume the source is useful because it was taken at the time.

● **Good, Level 2**
Answers focus on the ways in which the source is useful and not useful.

▲ **Excellent, Level 3**
Answers evaluate the usefulness of the source using its content, provenance and reliability.

Charitable hospitals

Many hospitals offered only basic care for the sick rather than the range of treatments we now expect, but some were aimed at specific groups of people. For example, sanatoriums were built to provide a healthy diet, fresh air and hygienic conditions, which patients with TB needed if they were to recover.

Since many hospitals were funded by charity, effective fundraising was vital. In 1912, Queen Alexandra, the mother of King George V (1910–1936), started a national Rose Day, on which volunteers sold roses to raise money for hospitals. The first Rose Day collected the equivalent of £2 million in today's money.

Source A: Alexandra Rose Day in 1912.

Source B: The outpatients department of St Paul's Eye Hospital, Liverpool, c1931, showing the problems charities faced in dealing with the number of people who needed help.

Improved access to health care	Improved standard of medical care available
By 1900, most cities had built infirmaries, fever houses and asylums to care for the poor. There were also local cottage hospitals and specialised sanatoriums, although most of these depended on charity for their funding.	Nurses were trained within a hospital.
1907: health visitors were introduced to visit mothers and help them care properly for their new babies.	By 1900, doctors had to have a university medical degree and to be accepted by the General Medical Council. They would have carried out dissections while training and have accompanied a doctor working on the hospital wards. Increasingly, doctors chose to become either a General Practitioner, who treated the community, or a doctor who worked in a hospital, usually specialising in one area of medicine.
1911 National Insurance Act: working men, their employers and the government all paid into a fund to cover doctors' fees and medical costs if a worker became ill, although it only applied to certain groups of men and did not cover their families.	1902 Midwives Act: midwives had to be properly trained and registered (it was hoped this would lower the rate of infant mortality).
	1919 Nursing Act: this set up the General Nursing Council to enforce high standards of training for nurses.

Increasing role for government

During the later part of the 19th century, the government had begun to take more responsibility for the public's health. This change of attitude was reinforced when over a third of the men who volunteered to fight in the British Army in the Boer War (1899–1902) were declared unfit and had to be turned away (this figure rose to nearly 90 per cent in slum areas in northern industrial cities such as Manchester). Since Britain relied on her army and navy to control a large empire, finding ways of improving the health of the working class became an important issue for the government, and war was therefore a factor in speeding up these changes.

There were improvements in how people could access care as well as improvements in the care available, with several key Acts being passed by the Liberal government in the period 1905–1911 (see table above and pages 84-85). However, there were fewer doctors in the poorer areas. Doctors could choose who to accept as their patients and they could refuse to give treatment if the patient could not pay them.

Source C: A slum in Whitechapel, London in the early 20th century; the poor standard of health of people living in such conditions put pressure on the government to take more action.

Activities

1 Make a list of government actions that had a role in improving medical care in the period 1900–1939.

2 Explain why many people continued to use traditional home remedies when more scientific treatment was possible.

Summary

Although the government was taking an increased role in improving the health of the nation, by 1939 there was still no national organisation offering the same level of care to everyone, and access to health care remained patchy.

4.8 Public health 1900–1948: the foundation of the Welfare State

Learning outcomes

By the end of this topic you should be able to:

● describe the improvements in access to health care in the early 20th century

● understand and evaluate the role of government in improving public health

Access to health care

Despite the public health reforms of the late 19th century, the standard of living among the poor remained very low. Surveys showing how difficult it was for the poor to afford decent housing and food were carried out by Charles Booth (in the period 1891–1903) and Seebohm Rowntree (in 1888–1901). Their work showed that the main reasons for poverty were ill-health and unemployment.

The Liberal government that was elected in 1905 began to pass laws that they hoped would improve health among the poor. The 1911 National Insurance Act was particularly important. Every worker earning less than £160 a year was expected to join the scheme, in which contributions by the worker, employer and government were made to fund:

● free medical treatment and medicine
● sick pay for up to six months and support payment while unemployed for up to 15 weeks.

Source A: Children in Bradford, 1907, having a bath to get rid of lice and fleas. This is an example of what actions some local authorities took to improve public health. As schooling had become compulsory, it meant that all children could be treated at the same time and place.

Source B: The beginnings of the Welfare State in the early 20th century.

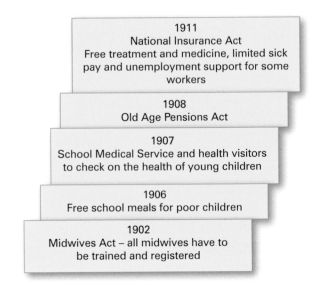

> **1911**
> National Insurance Act
> Free treatment and medicine, limited sick pay and unemployment support for some workers

> **1908**
> Old Age Pensions Act

> **1907**
> School Medical Service and health visitors to check on the health of young children

> **1906**
> Free school meals for poor children

> **1902**
> Midwives Act – all midwives have to be trained and registered

Although the 19th-century idea of laissez-faire was now less common, there was some resistance to the government's increasing involvement in people's lives. The first acts however concerned children and were more acceptable to many people. Some people resisted these welfare reforms because of the cost. Although he eventually succeeded, there was a crisis in parliament when the Chancellor, Lloyd George, needed to raise taxes to pay for the National Insurance Act, which was passed in 1911.

In 1919 the Ministry of Health was set up, which gave the government an overview of health care provision in the whole country. This was an important step in the government taking more responsibility for health, but actual provision continued to be a mixture of people paying for private care, local authorities providing some support and many hospitals relying on funding from charity. Sanatoria were built to care for people with TB, but there were still some problems.

- An epidemic of influenza in 1918–1919 showed that there were not enough free hospital places.
- Women and children were not covered by the National Insurance scheme and so they often delayed getting treatment because they could not afford to pay for a doctor.

However, the average life expectancy by 1931 had risen to 58 for males and 62 for females, and the government was doing much more to help improve the health of the nation.

For example:

- secondary school pupils received medical inspections
- free milk for poor primary schoolchildren was introduced in 1934
- health clinics gave vaccinations and sold baby food cheaply
- many hospitals were brought under the control of local authorities.

There was also a range of private health insurance schemes that could provide treatment for women, children and those men not covered by the government scheme.

These developments must also be seen in the context of the events you have read about on pages 42–44 and 62–66: a better understanding of disease, the development of a range of vaccinations and the development of better treatment for disease. These changes meant that people's expectations of medicine increased and they were far more willing than previously to accept government interaction.

There were also signs that the government was beginning to get more involved in educating people about healthcare and in trying to prevent disease. For example, the death of 3,000 children from diphtheria in 1938 shocked the government and led to a vaccination programme offering free immunisation. Although the vaccine for diphtheria had been developed about 25 years earlier, due to the cost and lack of knowledge, few people had been vaccinated until government intervention changed this. Cases of diphtheria in Britain dropped dramatically as a result.

The effects of the Second World War

The Second World War (1939–1945) had a major effect on people's awareness of the effects of poverty on health. People were shocked to find out that many children evacuated from towns were not used to running water or proper toilets and that they often had nits, lice or skin infections. This was an important factor in creating the desire for a higher standard of health after the war and the setting up of the **National Health Service** (NHS). However, the war also had an effect on people's diets. Food was rationed and fats and sugar were in short supply, while people were encouraged to eat more vegetables, with the result that some people, especially among the poor, found their health was actually better than it had been in the 1930s.

Activities

1 How far did public health improve during the early 20th century?
2 In what ways were the Liberal reforms of 1905–1911 a turning point in public health?
3 Research: find out how Lloyd George and the Liberals dealt with the opposition to the 'People's Budget', which was to raise money for the 1911 National Insurance Act.
4 What public health problems still existed by the start of the Second World War in 1939?
5 Which factor had the most effect on public health in the early 20th century – war or the role of government? Explain your answer.

Summary

During the early 20th century, central government intervened in a wide range of public health issues although local authorities were often responsible for actually carrying out many of the measures.

4.9 The creation of the NHS in 1948

Learning outcomes

By the end of this topic you should be able to:

- give reasons why the NHS was set up in 1948
- evaluate the role of Bevan in setting up the NHS
- explain why the NHS was a landmark event for public health in Britain

Source A: Health Minister Aneurin Bevan visiting one of the first patients being treated under the new NHS system in 1948.

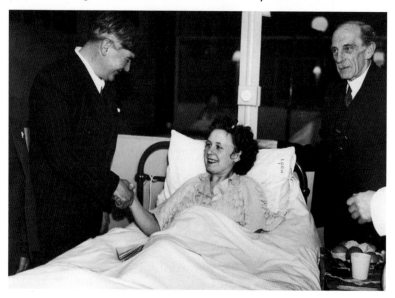

Why was the NHS set up?

We have already seen how government had become increasingly involved in health care provision in the first half of the 20th century. They had also become increasingly concerned about the inequalities of health care, especially once women got the vote in 1918.

The bombing raids in the Second World War (1939–1945) produced many casualties in the cities and the government set up a national Emergency Medical Service. This brought hospitals throughout the country under the control of the Ministry of Health.

Some new hospitals and 1,000 new operating theatres were built and additional equipment was provided.

The hospitals provided free treatment, a blood transfusion service was created and an ambulance service was set up. This all proved that government control over health care could work successfully.

When the war was over in 1945, the new Labour government made plans for a National Health Service (NHS), which was set up in 1948.

During the Second World War children had been evacuated from cities to stay in the countryside. Many people were shocked by the poverty they had grown up in. People wanted to create a 'New World' with better conditions for all.

By the mid-20th century, there was much more acceptance about the government being involved in people's lives.

What led to the setting up of the NHS in 1948?

There had been a need to organise hospitals and medical staff during the Second World War and this had worked successfully.

Significant medical breakthroughs meant that much more could be done for the sick.

The Beveridge Report in 1942 identified disease as a problem for the government to deal with after the Second World War.

The role of Aneurin Bevan

Aneurin Bevan was the Minister for Health in the post-war government. Whilst building on the work done in the Beveridge Report, his contribution to the foundation of the NHS was huge.

Bevan overcame opposition based on the cost of the NHS and also opposition from the British Medical Association, whose doctors were afraid they would lose money and their independence by being employed by the government. Bevan promised **consultants** in hospitals they could still treat private patients but he also issued pamphlets telling the public to check that their doctor was part of the NHS. This made doctors think they would lose patients if they didn't join the NHS.

The Beveridge report suggested the government should improve public health. → The new Labour government accepted these recommendations and began to plan the NHS.

Bevan publicised his ideas and persuaded patients they should ask to be registered as NHS patients. ← Bevan faced great opposition from many people, including doctors who did not want to lose their income from private patients.

This put pressure on doctors to join the NHS or lose their patients. → The NHS was launched in 1948.

The National Health Service, 1948

The creation of the NHS was a landmark event in public health in Britain. The government had gradually been taking more responsibility for the provision of sanitation, etc, and then had made attempts to improve the standard of living and access to health care. Now a national system that offered comprehensive care 'from cradle to grave' was put in place and funded by the government.

Taxes were used to pay for a wide range of care offered to people, including:

- the right to see a GP and to be referred to hospital
- treatment by dentists and opticians
- health care for pregnant women and young children
- ambulances and emergency treatment
- health care for the elderly.

This had a major impact on people's health. Previously only those covered by the national insurance system could see a GP free of charge.

Non-working women and children were not covered. Although many doctors set up schemes where people paid a small amount every week to cover the cost of treatment when it was needed, many people still could not afford this. The cost of the doctor's visit and the medicine would often make people delay seeking treatment until they were seriously ill. Through the NHS people could see their doctor and get treatment at an early stage of an illness and therefore had a better chance of recovery, and access to professional nursing care. These changes marked a significant improvement in the accessibility of medical care and facilities, and benefited enormously the poorest people in society.

At first all treatments were entirely free, and the government believed the cost of health care would actually go down because so much illness would be prevented. However, the expense of running the NHS was soon much higher than expected and **prescription charges** were introduced in 1951.

Activities

1. How far do you think the creation of the NHS was a turning point in the nature of government involvement in public health?
2. Explain who you think made the greater contribution to improving public health – Chadwick in the 19th century or Bevan in the 20th century.

Summary

The creation of the NHS was extremely important for improved access to health care for all. Bevan is an example of a key individual who impacted on public health reform.

4.10 Public health 1900 to present day: prevention and education

Learning outcomes

By the end of this topic you should be able to:

- give examples of how the government's role in public health has expanded since 1900
- evaluate the extent and nature of the change in government role in public health after 1948

Developments in education and prevention

The poster below shows how far understanding of the causes of disease had progressed by the 1930s. It also shows that the government now accepted that it had a role to play in educating and encouraging people to stay healthy – in other words, the government was starting to take more of a role in trying to prevent illness.

Source A: A poster produced by the government in the 1930s.

As a deeper understanding of both disease and the effects of people's lifestyle on health has grown, this has led to a wider role for government, emphasising prevention of illness. For example:

- developments in vaccinations, such as Jonas Salk's polio vaccine in the mid-1950s, and the introduction of a vaccine in 2008 against cervical cancer
- government campaigns and laws on health issues such as smoking
- government promotion of healthy diets
- better disposal of rubbish and treatment of sewage
- laws to reduce air and water pollution, for example the 1956 Clean Air Act, which dealt with the problem of smog (a mixture of fog and smoke from coal fires, industry and car fumes)
- laws to improve people's working conditions, for example health and safety regulations about asbestos in the workplace
- provision of environmental health officers to inspect restaurants, cafes and bars
- strict laws on food safety in 1990 after outbreaks of salmonella, E. coli poisoning, and BSE in cattle.

Government action on smoking

Smoking proved very popular in the mid-20th century when cigarettes became very cheap. However, in the mid-1960s it became clear that there were links between smoking and cancer, heart disease and many other health issues.

- In 1962 the Royal College of Physicians called for a ban on tobacco advertising.
- The government began taxing cigarettes heavily.
- Since 1971 packets of cigarettes have carried a health warning.
- In 2004 it was reported that over half a million admissions to hospital and 1 in 6 deaths were as a result of smoking.
- In 2005 a ban was placed on most forms of tobacco advertising.
- Smoking in public places was banned in 2006 in Scotland and in 2007 in England and Wales.

Communication

Government action has also been taken over obesity in school children and there is concern about binge drinking alcohol. In all these cases, communication has played an important role in the government campaign, with messages on the products, posters and television campaigns to raise awareness of the effects on people's health of their behaviour. When new health risks appear, the government has a key role in providing information to the public and support for sufferers. When HIV/AIDS was recognised as a significant risk to health in the 1980s, the government funded a national information campaign under the slogan: 'AIDS: don't die of ignorance'. Many believe this campaign is the reason why HIV/AIDS rates for the UK have been relatively small compared to elsewhere.

Public health and private companies

Private companies are increasingly involved in public health. For example, the responsibility for the provision of water has now been passed to private companies but the fact that many of the pipes are over 100 years old and need repairs or to be replaced causes problems for the water companies, who are reluctant to carry out the repairs because of the cost.

Source B: The chef Jamie Oliver led a campaign to encourage children to choose healthier options for school dinners, which influenced government action.

FASCINATING FACT

It is estimated that there are 60 million rats in Britain – and that a 24 per cent increase over the last few years is partly the result of fast food being thrown away on streets. Another reason for the increase is that water companies have not set as many traps for rats in their sewers as they used to. A female rat will live about 18 months and can have a litter every month – producing a potential 2,000 rats within a single year.

Activities

1 What additional responsibilities in public health has the government taken on since the second half of the 20th century?

2 How far do you think the government should regulate health issues such as sex education or the availability of alcohol?

3 How far do you think that aspects of public health being controlled by private companies could lead to regress (a lowering of standards) in public health?

Summary

Throughout the 20th century, but particularly in the second half, the government took on an increasingly active role in attempts to prevent ill health and in educating people to take more responsibility for their own health. There has also been an increased involvement of private companies in public health.

4.11 Other developments and implications of modern healthcare

90

Learning outcomes

By the end of this topic you should be able to:

- explain some of the problems facing the NHS and medicine today
- understand that science and technology have not always led to progress within medicine

The pharmaceutical industry

The late 19th century saw the beginnings of a pharmaceutical industry as companies such as Beecham and Boots began making and selling prepared mixtures and pills to cure illnesses. Few of these first pills did any good (and some actually did harm) but, as progress in science led to the discoveries of first magic bullets and then antibiotics which successfully cured disease, pharmaceutical companies began to play an increasingly important role. They:

- employed and financed scientists and researchers to find other cures and remedies
- used and developed technology and industry to mass-produce remedies
- used advertising to make people aware of their products and buy them.

Through financial backing, and providing scientists with the equipment they need, the pharmaceutical industry has played an important role in finding new cures and treatments and making them available. However, the industry has created some problems.

The pharmaceutical industry expects to make a profit and therefore many companies produce different versions of the same basic pill, for example there are many branded versions of paracetamol. Although each new drug is tested before it is licensed for sale, there can be problems during the tests or unforeseen side-effects.

For example, in the 1960s, a new drug called thalidomide was used to prevent morning sickness in pregnant women but it was found that it affected the growth of the unborn baby and, in particular, the development of the arms and legs (see the photo below).

Source A: A child affected by thalidomide.

Ethical questions

As well as concerns about the side-effects of new drugs, there is a lot of debate about whether scientists should 'play God' and use their knowledge of genetics to change people's bodies. Some research depends on experiments with human embryos; others combine animal and human cells together; and cloning has already been used on animals. The medical potential of these experiments is colossal – but many people object to them on religious and moral grounds or from fear that the side-effects could be equally far-reaching.

> **FASCINATING FACT**
> The NHS currently takes up about a quarter of all government spending, and is the largest employer in Europe and the third largest employer in the world.

The increasing cost of medicine and treatment

The rising cost of the NHS soon became a problem for government. It is now a major problem, as costs increase every year. This is because:

- As people live longer, they are more likely to develop problems needing treatment.
- Improvements in medicine mean people expect a greater range of treatment, for example, kidney dialysis, heart surgery, care for premature babies, cancer therapy.
- New drugs can help many conditions, but the costs can be very high.
- Treatment is more complex and equipment more expensive, with new technology such as MRI scans.
- Staff costs are high because of increased training for doctors and nurses, increased wages for highly trained staff, and nursing care while patients recover from treatment.
- As we saw on pages 88–89, the role of the NHS widened in the later 20th century to include more prevention methods as well as treatments.

A return to private healthcare?

Long waiting lists for treatment developed in the late 20th century, with rising demand for treatment from a growing, aging population, and many people's conditions deteriorated before they could get the specialist help they needed.

As a result, private companies offering medical services have grown in recent years (as has private medical insurance), so many who can afford it choose to pay for at least some healthcare. Many GPs and consultants now offer private work as well as their work for the NHS.

In recent years, GPs have been encouraged to offer a wider range of care, and many now have a nurse attached to their practice and run specialised clinics. However, changes in the way GPs are funded by the state have meant that few of them now offer an emergency service at night or at weekends – this is usually organised by an agency instead.

In 2008, the NHS celebrated its 60th anniversary, but there is much discussion about whether it should continue in its current form or if there should be radical changes to the system.

Activities

1. Use the illustration showing the different aspects of the NHS to explain how extensive the role of the NHS has been in improving public health.

2. Write two short articles for a newspaper: one article to celebrate the achievements and successes of the NHS 1948–2008, and another to criticize its shortcomings and disappointments.

3. Explain the positive and negative effects of the pharmaceutical industry on medicine.

Summary

The significant improvements in healthcare and treatment in the 20th century have not been without some problems, such as financial costs and ethical issues.

4.12 Change and continuity: how much has medicine changed since 1900?

Learning outcome

By the end of this topic you should be able to:

- give examples of changes in medicine since 1900

- understand that changes happen at different rates and change isn't always positive

1990	Human Genome Project was launched – an international effort to map all of the genes in the human body.
1994	The first breast cancer gene was discovered.
1995	The discovery of a gene linked to Parkinson's disease led to hope of future treatment and a cure for this condition.
1996	Scottish scientists created a sheep named Dolly using cells cloned from an adult sheep.
1997	The discovery was made that stem cells can be used for repairs to damaged or faulty tissues in the body.
1998	A rough draft of the human genome map was produced, showing the locations of more than 30,000 genes.

How change happens

Many factors have led to changes in medicine, and they often act in combination. For example, some developments in science and technology happen only because the government is prepared to fund them.

Factors can have both positive and negative effects. For example, war provides opportunities to experiment and speeds up some developments – the First World War gave an added urgency to the search to find a way to store blood because it would save many injured soldiers who needed transfusions. However, war can hold back other developments because it diverts money and research away from work that is less obviously relevant (see pages 76–77).

Speed of change

You should also remember that changes happen at different speeds. One scientific or technological breakthrough can lead to several others in a very short space of time, such as happened with the rapid developments in vaccines or genetics. Yet these discoveries can take a long time to have an effect on the treatment people receive.

Change and progress

When antibiotics were discovered it was thought that infection had been completely conquered, but some types of bacteria have become resistant to these drugs. The 'superbugs' MRSA and C. difficile have caused deaths in some British hospitals in the early 21st century, and this has led the British government to insist on new standards of hygiene in the NHS. Scientists have also been working on new methods to combat these infections. This shows us that progress in medicine is sometimes slow and not as complete as we believe it is.

Source A: Dolly died after six years, half the usual life expectancy of this breed of sheep. She was then stuffed and put on display at the Royal Museum of Scotland.

Activities

1. Study Source B, the photograph of a modern hospital ward. How many developments can you identify that show changes since 1900 century, for example:

   a) improved knowledge and understanding of illness?

   b) improved standards of hygiene?

   c) greater use of technology?

2. Draw a timeline to show the major developments in medicine from 1900 to the present day.

3. On your timeline, colour code: a) developments that helped to treat illness and b) developments that helped to prevent illness. Use a dotted line to show any developments that are directly connected to each other.

4. How did war help the development of blood transfusions and penicillin?

5. Why does religion seem to have so much less impact on medicine in the modern period than the medieval period?

6. Draw an ideas map showing the links between the roles of war, government, science and technology, and key individuals' attitudes and beliefs in the modern period.

Source B: A modern NHS hospital ward.

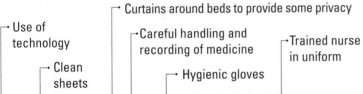

Use of technology

Curtains around beds to provide some privacy

Careful handling and recording of medicine

Trained nurse in uniform

Clean sheets

Hygienic gloves

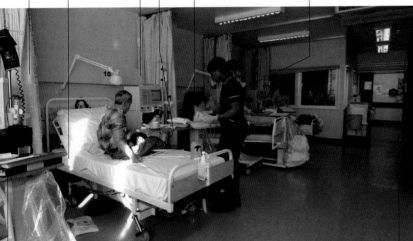

Patient's medical notes at end of each bed

Visitors limited to control infection

examzone

Build better answers

How far was the progress that was made in medical care in the second half of the 20th century due to the increased role of government? Explain your answer.   (16 marks)

You may use the following in your answer:

• The setting up of the NHS

• Advances in science and technology

You must also include information of your own.

 Basic, Level 1

Answers only offer general comments on how medical care improved.

Good, Level 2

Answers describe how medical care improved and the government's role in this.

Better, Level 3

Answers provide some analysis of factors which led to progress, including the role of government, with some support from relevant material.

Excellent, Level 4

Answers provide detailed and sustained analysis of a range of factors which led to progress and evaluate the role of government against other factors. Points are well-supported by relevant material.

Make sure you write accurately – there are three extra marks available for spelling, grammar and punctuation in these questions.

Summary

The period from 1900 to the present has been a time of many changes, but these changes have happened at different speeds and have not always led to progress.

4.13 How do historians research a controversy?

Learning outcome

By the end of this topic you should be able to:
- understand the way a historian evaluates sources when researching a controversy

There are often controversies in history where the evidence offers different views and opinions. This investigation will consider the case of DNA, which you have already studied on pages 78–79. You are asked to consider whether Rosalind Franklin should receive more recognition for her role in its discovery.

examzone

Watch out!

The most common misunderstanding from students if sources contradict each other is either:
- to assume that one source is completely wrong and the other is completely right, or
- to try to find a compromise, where both sources are 'half right'.

The key, as always, is to evaluate each source and think about whether the author:
- might be mistaken
- has a reason to be deliberately misleading
- can offer proof to show that their version is correct.

Rosalind Franklin

Rosalind Franklin
- Born 1920.
- Studied chemistry at Cambridge University.
- In 1951 accepted a position at King's College London, working on the new technique of X-ray crystallography and studying DNA.
- Relations with Wilkins were difficult because he was already working on this topic and expected her to join his team.
- Took photographs of DNA.

Crick and Watson, with their model of the structure of DNA

Francis Crick
- Born 1916 in England.
- Trained as a physicist.
- Shared office with James Watson from 1951.
- Began to research molecular biology and genetics.

James Watson
- Born in 1928 in America.
- Moved to Cambridge University 1951.
- Researched DNA.

Source A: Rosalind Franklin's X-ray photo of DNA.

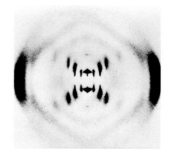

Maurice Wilkins – awarded the Nobel Prize along with Crick and Watson

Maurice Wilkins
- Born 1916, New Zealand.
- Moved to England when six years old.
- Worked at King's College, London.
- Expert in X-ray photography.
- Friends with Crick and Watson.

Stages in the discovery of DNA

1 Crick and Watson teamed up to try to build a model of DNA.

2 They made use of other specialisms and were very interested to hear of Wilkins' and Franklin's work.

3 Franklin looked at their model of DNA and pointed out something in their work that her photographs showed was a mistake.

4 Franklin had given Wilkins all her data to use as he wished. When Watson visited Wilkins in London, Wilkins showed him Franklin's clearest photograph.

5 Crick and Watson used Franklin's photograph to help them complete their model.

6 Franklin wrote up her findings and published them at exactly the same time as Wilkins, and Crick and Watson.

The Nobel Prize in 1962 was shared between Crick, Watson and Wilkins – but not Franklin because the Nobel Prize is not awarded posthumously and she had died four years earlier. This means that she tended not to receive the same recognition as the others initially.

Cases such as these can be approached in a number of ways.

- The historian may want to assess the role played by each person – for example, would Crick and Watson have discovered the structure of DNA without Franklin's photograph?
- The investigation may focus on how the discovery was seen at the time – why did Crick and Watson get the credit for the discovery of DNA's structure?

So how does the historian research a controversy? Just as with any other enquiry, the historian must look at all the available sources and evaluate them carefully in order to establish the facts without being influenced by other people's opinions.

Evidence about the role of Franklin in the discovery of the structure of DNA

Source B: From the outline of a TV programme about Franklin.

Today, nearly all scientists agree that the hard evidence used to support Crick, Watson and Wilkins' theory about DNA was based on the work of Rosalind Franklin, a brilliant molecular biologist and crystallographer.

Source C: A comment from an article by Crick in 1974.

Rosalind Franklin was only two steps away from the solution but she was about to give up working on DNA. However, I don't think the discovery would have been delayed very much because Wilkins was going to work full time on the problem.

Franklin was not part of Crick and Watson's team but her photograph was helpful in suggesting the shape of the DNA double helix. However it is not clear whether it was a crucial breakthrough – Pauling in America was also researching the structure of DNA and seemed close to a solution even without Franklin's photographs.

Activities

1 What evidence contemporary to their work might be available that could show the contribution made by each of the four individuals, Crick, Watson, Wilkins and Franklin, to the discovery of the structure of DNA?

2 How do you think historians should treat evidence from these people if it comes from a later time, for example, Crick's comment about Rosalind Franklin in an article in 1974, shown in Source C?

Medicine and public health in Britain, c50AD to the present day: summary

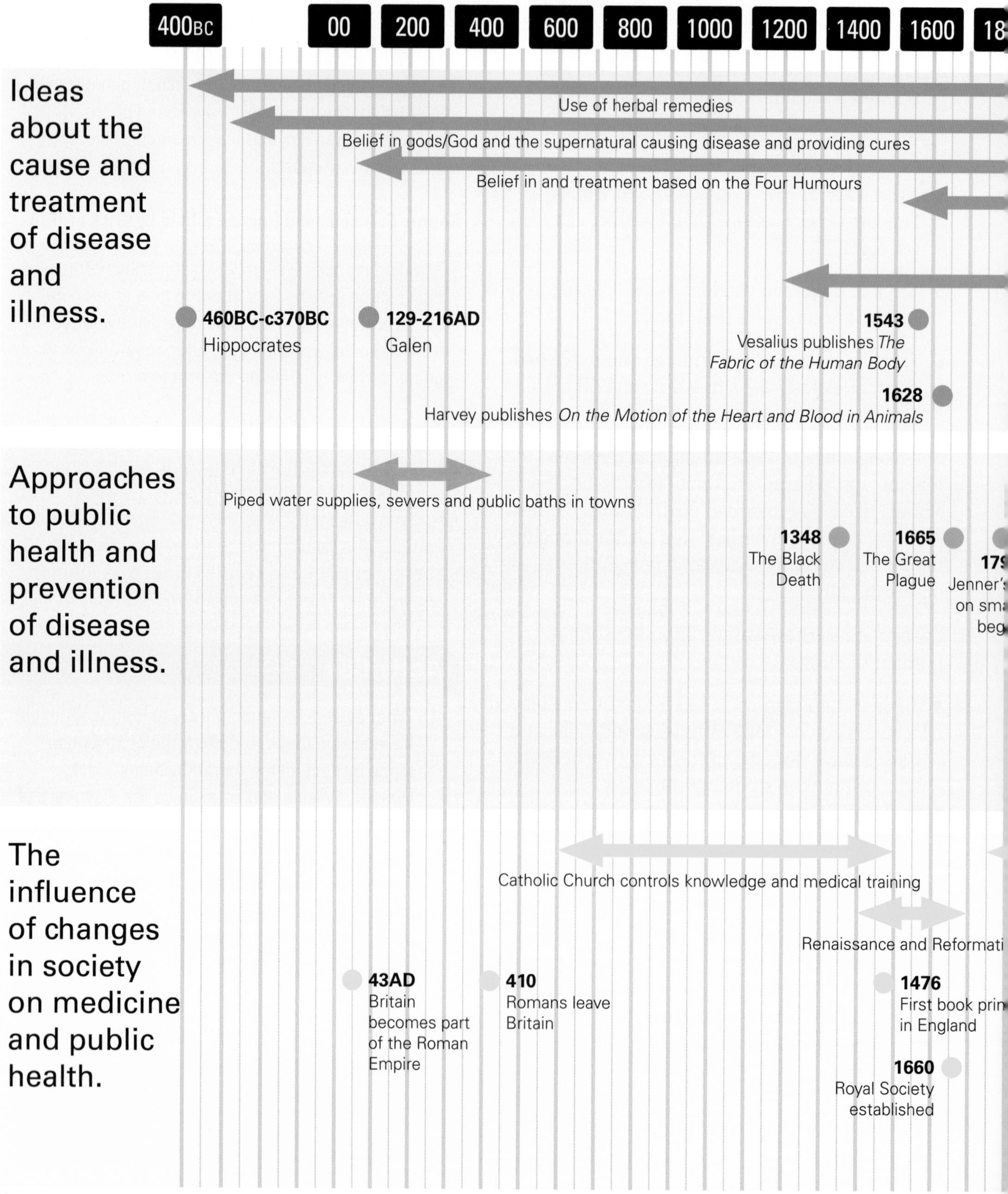

| 400BC | 00 | 200 | 400 | 600 | 800 | 1000 | 1200 | 1400 | 1600 | 18 |

Ideas about the cause and treatment of disease and illness.

Use of herbal remedies

Belief in gods/God and the supernatural causing disease and providing cures

Belief in and treatment based on the Four Humours

460BC–c370BC Hippocrates

129-216AD Galen

1543 Vesalius publishes *The Fabric of the Human Body*

1628 Harvey publishes *On the Motion of the Heart and Blood in Animals*

Approaches to public health and prevention of disease and illness.

Piped water supplies, sewers and public baths in towns

1348 The Black Death

1665 The Great Plague

179 Jenner's on sma beg

The influence of changes in society on medicine and public health.

Catholic Church controls knowledge and medical training

Renaissance and Reformati

43AD Britain becomes part of the Roman Empire

410 Romans leave Britain

1476 First book prin in England

1660 Royal Society established

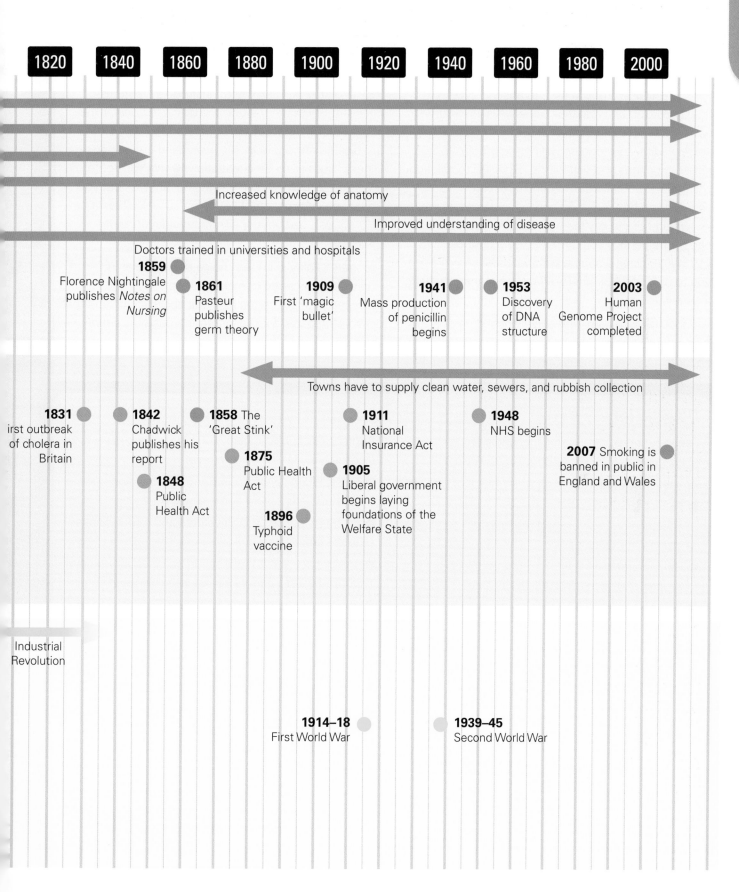

1820 **1840** **1860** **1880** **1900** **1920** **1940** **1960** **1980** **2000**

Increased knowledge of anatomy

Improved understanding of disease

Doctors trained in universities and hospitals

1859
Florence Nightingale
publishes *Notes on
Nursing*

1861
Pasteur
publishes
germ theory

1909
First 'magic
bullet'

1941
Mass production
of penicillin
begins

1953
Discovery
of DNA
structure

2003
Human
Genome Project
completed

Towns have to supply clean water, sewers, and rubbish collection

1831
irst outbreak
of cholera in
Britain

1842
Chadwick
publishes his
report

1858 The
'Great Stink'

1875
Public Health
Act

1911
National
Insurance Act

1948
NHS begins

2007 Smoking is
banned in public in
England and Wales

1848
Public
Health Act

1896
Typhoid
vaccine

1905
Liberal government
begins laying
foundations of the
Welfare State

Industrial
Revolution

1914–18
First World War

1939–45
Second World War

KnowZone Medicine and public health in Britain, c50AD to the present day

Introduction

For the Unit 1 exam, you have to answer five questions. The first question will always ask you what two sources reveal about an aspect of medicine or public health. The sources will normally be from two different periods and you will be expected to talk about change or continuity. The second question will give you a choice between two options and will test your knowledge of the key features and characteristics of one of the periods you have studied. For question 3, you will be given a source and the question will ask you to evaluate how useful it is to a historian studying a certain topic.

You then have to complete either question 4 or 5 *and* either question 6 or 7. Question 4/5 will be about factors impacting on change and/or continuity.

Question 6/7 will ask you to analyse key features of an event or period of study and evaluate how far they contributed to progress in understanding disease, medical treatment or public health and preventing illness. Both of these questions will give you some information that you can use in your answer, but you must use information of your own as well. Question 6/7 will also test your spelling, punctuation and grammar.

As there is only a limited choice of questions in the exam, you need to make sure you have good knowledge of all the topics in the specification and that you are prepared for the different types of question that are asked.

Checklist

The key themes throughout the whole unit are:

Ideas about the cause and treatment of disease and illness. For example:

- Beliefs about God and the supernatural and their influence on beliefs about the cause of disease and treatments for disease.
- Hippocrates' and Galen's natural explanation for the causes of disease and their treatments.
- The impact of the Renaissance on beliefs about the causes of disease.
- The move towards a scientific understanding of the causes of disease and genetic conditions, and related treatments.

Approaches to public health and prevention of disease and illness. For example:

- Public health systems in Roman Britain and how they helped prevent some disease.
- Medieval public health systems and methods used to prevent illness.
- The impact of industrialisation on disease and new public health systems set up to tackle them.
- The setting up of the NHS in 1948 and its changing role in preventing as well as treating illness.

The influence of changes in society on medicine and public health. For example:

- The impact of Roman occupation and withdrawal.
- The influence of religion and the Church during the Middle Ages and the impact of the declining influence of the Church.
- The impact of the Renaissance.
- The impact of the industrial revolution – the increasing size of urban areas and living and working conditions, and the development of technology.
- Changing attitudes towards the role and intervention of government in public health.

Revision activity

Go back through your notes and through this book and summarise the key points in a table like this:

Period	Ideas about the cause of disease	Approaches to treatment	Public health and prevention	Changes in society	Amount of progress
50–450 Roman Britain	Four Humours Supernatural Bad air				
450–1350 Early Middle Ages				War / invasions / unstable rule Increasing influence of Church	
1350–1500 Later Middle Ages		Herbal remedies Religious / superstitious cures Bloodletting and purging			
1500–1750 Renaissance				Beginnings of a scientific approach Church reducing control	
1750–1900 Industrial revolution			After 1850, increase of clean water provision, rubbish collection, sewers, etc		
1900–present Modern					Huge changes in both ideas about causes of disease, prevention and treatments. Medicine can now deal with/ cure many types of illness, but not all.

Student tips

When I was revising my teacher said it was important to know the order of events, so I wrote out lots of timelines. I also did ideas maps to show all the different factors that affected a change and I found it helpful to get a picture that showed a key aspect of medicine in a period and to annotate it.

Mini exam paper

Question 1

Study Sources A and B.

Source A: A woodcut showing flagellants whipping themselves so they wouldn't catch the Black Death.

You only need to use these two sources to give a good answer. Notice the focus on changes in the question – you'll need to explain the difference between the methods shown in the two pictures.

Think about the question. How are people trying to prevent themselves getting the Black Death in Source A?

Source B: Hand wash at the entrance of a 21st century hospital ward.

Think about what Source B is showing – what does this show about how people think disease is caused today?

What do Sources A and B show about changes in the beliefs about the causes of disease?

Explain your answer, using Sources A and B and your own knowledge. (8 marks)

Mark scheme

Examiners have strict guidance on how to award your marks in the exam. For the question we are looking at, it would be like this.

Basic – some simple statements. These will generalise about changes in beliefs about the causes of disease without supporting evidence from the sources or own knowledge of the context. Alternatively, these answers will give details about the sources, perhaps including some own knowledge, but without addressing the changes in belief they show.

Good – more development statements. These will discuss changes in beliefs in the causes of disease and offer some details from the sources and/or from own knowledge in support.

Excellent – developed analysis. These will make inferences about the nature or extent of change in beliefs about the causes of disease, based on explicit use of both the sources and support by own knowledge of the historical context of the sources.

Study Sources A and B. What do Sources A and B show about changes in the beliefs about the causes of disease? Explain your answer, using Sources A and B and your own knowledge. (8 marks)

Source A: A 1485 woodcut showing flagellants whipping themselves.

Source B: Hand wash at the entrance of a 21st century hospital ward.

Student answer	Comments	Improved student answer
Source A shows flagellants whipping themselves so they wouldn't catch the Black Death. They did this because they wanted to show God how sorry they were for their bad behaviour, so he would show mercy on them and not make them ill.	This answer offers a good explanation of what the source is showing, but doesn't link this to what people believed caused disease at that time. You need to be explicit in your answers!	Source A shows flagellants whipping themselves so they wouldn't catch the Black Death. They did this because they believed that God caused disease. They wanted to show God how sorry they were for their bad behaviour, so he would show mercy on them and not make them ill. By the 21st century, beliefs about the causes of disease were more scientific.
Source B shows hygienic hand wash, which is used to stop people spreading their germs and diseases when they visit patients in hospital.	Again, there is good knowledge of what the source is showing, but this isn't related to the question. The student needs to explain how the sources illustrate the different beliefs about the causes of disease. Also, the student doesn't add any of their own knowledge to enhance their answer.	This is shown in Source B, which illustrates the modern knowledge that many diseases are caused by germs and that hygiene is important for stopping the spread of germs. This indicates a move from supernatural to scientific beliefs in the causes of disease.

⭐ exam zone
Build better answers

The boxes below show two different periods. Choose one and describe the key features of medical training during that period. (6 marks)
- The later Middle Ages
- The nineteenth century

Student answer	Comments	Improved student answer
In the 19th century, medical training began to improve as doctors had to pass exams before they would be given a certificate. However, as you didn't need a certificate to practise as a doctor that didn't make lots of difference! It was after 1858 that the government passed the General Medical Act that said that all qualified doctors had to be registered with the General Medical Council.	This doesn't really answer the question at all! The question asks for the key features of medical training – this is just about qualifications and the professionalisation of doctor's training.	In the 19th century, medical training for doctors began to improve. In 1800, doctor's training was still largely based on theory – reading medical books and studying written work by other doctors, usually at a university or medical school. However, gradually it became more practical, with the observation of qualified doctors and limited practical work in teaching hospitals. Students also began to use microscopes to understand more about illness, so training became more scientific. Many medical students began carrying out their own dissections of human bodies to find out more about human anatomy for themselves rather than just from books.
Also in the 19th century, there began to be proper training for nurses after the work of Florence Nightingale in Scutari during the Crimean War. She taught nurses how to keep patients and hospital facilities clean, which was important in stopping infection.	This is a little better, as is does include some features of the training – teaching nurses about cleanliness. However, far more detail of the features of training is needed.	For the first time in the 19th century, there began to be proper training for nurses after the work of Florence Nightingale in Scutari during the Crimean War. Nurses were taught practical skills such as how to keep hospital facilities clean, which was important in stopping infection. They were also taught how to keep patients and their wounds clean.

How useful is this chart to a historian who is investigating the work of physicians in the Middle Ages? Use Source A and your own knowledge to explain your answer. (8 marks)

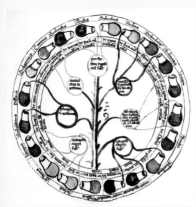

Source A: Medieval urine wheel. Labelled in Latin, this 15th century diagram shows some of the possible colours of urine (outer edge of circle) to help doctors diagnose urine-related diseases. Artwork from Fasciculus Medicinae, a collection of medieval medical manuscripts, published in Europe, that date from 1491.

Student answer	Comments	Improved student answer
This source is very useful because it's from a medical book for physicians in the 14th century.	This really just repeats information in the caption and question and you cannot assume that a source is useful just because it was produced/used at the time. The usefulness of a source depends on what the historian is investigating, so the student needs to state this in their answer.	This source is a urine chart from a medical book for physicians in the 14th century. It is a useful source for historians studying medical treatment in the Middle Ages because it shows one part of a physician's work – diagnosing what was wrong with a patient.
Urine charts were used by doctors to find out what was wrong with people – they would examine their patient's urine and compare it to the chart. After that, they would prescribe some treatment. This chart is proof that doctors did this as it is in a book that doctors would have used during their training and when they examined people.	The student uses their own knowledge well to explain how urine charts were used. However, there is no attempt to explain the limitations of the source or examine the source's provenance or reliability.	Urine charts were used by doctors to find out what was wrong with people – they would examine their patient's urine and compare it to the chart. After that they would prescribe some treatment. This chart is proof that doctors did this as it is in a book that doctors would have used during their training and when they examined people. However, this is just from one book – there is no information on how widely used this book was. The historian would need to know more information about the book itself to prove that it is a genuine medical book, commonly used by physicians at the time. Also, it only shows one aspect of the work done by doctors – therefore the historian would find this source useful but only as part of a greater selection of sources giving information on the work physicians did at this time.

Build better answers

Why did the discovery of a vaccination for smallpox in 1796 not lead to more preventative treatments? (12 marks)
You may use the following in your answer:
- Edward Jenner
- Cowpox

You must also include information of your own.

Student answer	Comments	Improved student answer
Edward Jenner was a doctor in Gloucestershire. He tested the idea that, if people had caught cowpox, then they did not catch smallpox. He carried out tests on many people by injecting them with cowpox. They became ill, but recovered quickly. He then injected them with smallpox and they didn't get it at all!	The student shows good use of their own knowledge in describing Jenner's work, but this isn't really answering the question so far.	Edward Jenner used scientific methods to test the idea that if people caught cowpox they would not catch smallpox. He proved this idea worked by injecting people with cowpox and then smallpox. However, Jenner's work only proved there was a link between cowpox and smallpox – he hadn't found links between any other diseases.
He had to pay to publish his findings himself as the Royal Society wouldn't. Initially, patients and doctors were reluctant to try it. However, after a while, the government gave Jenner some money so he could promote his vaccination and give it to more people. Eventually people believed it worked, although it took the government making vaccination compulsory for it to really have a big effect on reducing smallpox. In 1979, the World Health Organization announced that smallpox had been wiped out.	Again, there is more description of Jenner's work and the factors that made it successful in eventually getting rid of smallpox – but there is nothing about why this didn't lead to preventative treatments for other diseases.	Jenner's work did not lead to other treatments because he gained no understanding in what caused smallpox and therefore had got no further in understanding the causes of disease generally. It was not until Pasteur's germ theory in 1861 that there was a real breakthrough in understanding the causes of disease and this directly led to more vaccinations to prevent illness and cures for treating them.
However, Jenner had only found a link between smallpox and cowpox, so it didn't work for any other disease.	Finally, this offers something to answer the question – but it is far too little to do well alone!	In conclusion, Jenner's vaccination was successful in preventing smallpox but, because he did not know the reasons why it worked, it couldn't be used to develop vaccinations for other diseases.

How far was the progress made in medicine by the Romans continued in the Middle Ages in England? Explain your answer.
(16 marks + 3 marks for SPaG)
You may use the following in your answer:
- Public health
- Medical training

You must also include information of your own.

Student answer	Comments	Improved student answer
The Romans made a great deal of progress in medicine. They thought hygiene was important and they made great advances in public health. They used aqueducts and lead pipes to deliver clean water to towns. They also built sewers to take the waste away from the living areas in places such as York and Bath.	This makes some valid points about what the Romans did to improve hygiene, although it could have explained how clean water and the removal of waste was progress for medicine.	The Romans made a great deal of progress in medicine. They thought hygiene was important and they made great advances in public health. They used aqueducts and lead pipes to deliver clean water to towns, which would improve people's hygiene and would also cut down on diseases spread by unclean water. They also built sewers to take the waste away from the living areas in places like York and Bath, which was important as some diseases are spread through infected sewage.
The Romans built public baths that everyone could use and, at the baths, people would exercise and then have the sweat scraped off them, then go into the pool. There would be several pools, each one getting hotter, but at the end they would plunge into the cold pool.	This section of the answer provides a description of the public baths but does not link any of this information to the question so would get very little credit for it. There is nothing about how this compared to the Middle Ages, which is the focus of the question.	The Romans built public baths that were very cheap so that everyone could use them. A higher standard of hygiene helped to reduce the spread of disease, even though the Romans did not know why. This all ended when the Romans left Britain c410 AD and these things fell into disuse, so the progress made by the Romans in public health was not continued into the Middle Ages.
This all ended when the Romans left Britain in c410 AD and these things fell into disuse, so the progress made by the Romans was not continued in the Middle Ages.	Again, there is an understanding that public health and hygiene are linked to medicine, but it is not explained. It has very little extra knowledge and is focused on public health rather than medicine. The answer should make use of the second bullet point in the question plus add some of own knowledge. The student's spelling, punctuation and grammar is good but fairly basic.	Medical training in Roman times was based on the ideas and works of Galen. This was lost for a time after the Romans left, but emerged again in the later part of the early Middle Ages. However, some of these ideas were wrong, so it is not clear whether this aspect of medicine was actually progress. Herbal remedies and supernatural ideas were prominent in Roman times and continued throughout the Middle Ages. Again, some of these worked but many didn't so it cannot be regarded as progress.

The transformation of surgery c1845–c1918

Introduction

This unit looks at a key period in surgery, when major changes were made.

It is separated into the following sections:

- dealing with pain
- dealing with infection
- dealing with blood loss
- factors influencing these developments.

It is also the unit where you need to develop your understanding of source enquiry skills. This section of the book will therefore give you information about advances in surgery during this period and each section will also be followed by work that will help you to develop your source enquiry skills.

The examination questions in this unit usually follow a pattern testing the following skills:

- inference
- purpose
- source comprehension
- source evaluation for reliability
- using sources to reach a judgement.

You will need to combine your source analysis skills with your own knowledge for all these, with the exception of questions about inference.

Remember that you will also be tested on your spelling, punctuation and grammar. So it would be a good idea to jot down tricky medical words and learn how to spell them correctly!

Source A: An etching of an operation in 1793 by Rowlandson.

Source B: A carbolic spray, used to prevent infection during an operation in the 1870s.

1846	1846	1847	1848	1853	1861	1867
Morton used ether to anaesthetise a patient in the USA.	Liston used ether during amputation in Britain.	Simpson used chloroform.	Hannah Greener died while receiving chloroform.	Queen Victoria received chloroform during childbirth.	Pasteur's germ theory.	Lister use carbolic a

Source C: A photograph of an operation in 1900.

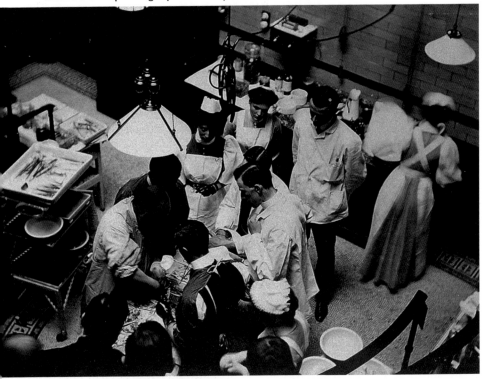

Source D: A barber's shop showing a red and white striped pole.

Far from being a respected medical person, the surgeon in the Middle Ages was usually a barber – who happened to do surgery as well because he had a collection of sharp knives! Right up to the late 20th century, a traditional barber's shop used to have a red and white striped pole outside, which symbolised blood and bandages, to remind people that they also used to do surgical operations.

Although surgery had become more scientific by the end of the 18th century, thanks to the work of John Hunter (see page 41), people usually had to be desperate before they agreed to have an operation. They knew they would suffer great pain, and many patients died during an operation. However, even if they survived the operation, many patients still died later from infection or blood loss.

Activities

1 Look at Rowlandson's picture of an operation at the end of the 18th century (Source A). What effect do you think this picture would have on someone who needed surgery?

2 Now look at the picture of an operation in 1900 (Source C). How many changes can you identify?

1877	1878	1901	1905	1916	1916
...ter became ...ofessor of Surgery ...King's College ...spital, London, and ...blicised his ideas ...ut antiseptics.	Koch developed the steam steriliser.	Landsteiner identified blood groups.	Novocaine used as an anaesthetic.	Rous and Turner developed a way of storing blood.	Gilles set up a plastic surgery unit at Aldershot.

5.1 Surgery and anaesthetics in the 19th century

Learning outcomes

By the end of this topic you should be able to:

- understand and explain some of the problems involved in surgery
- explain the importance of speed in operations and understand that this need for speed caused further problems

Amputation: The cutting off of a limb – for example, an arm or a leg – from the body

Anaesthetic: A substance that affects your nervous system so that you are less aware of sensation and don't feel pain

Tourniquet: Something that is tied around a part of the body to put pressure on a blood vessel and stop the loss of blood

The most common sorts of surgical operations in the 19th century were **amputations**, where an arm or leg had to be cut off. This was a fairly straightforward procedure but extremely painful and many people died from blood loss or from infection.

Another operation that was carried out was 'cutting for the stone' in the bladder. This was where there had been some problem inside the body leading to a 'stone' forming inside the bladder, similar to a kidney stone or gall stone. It was an extremely painful condition but since it was in the bladder, it was not deep inside the body. Therefore the surgeon could make a cut at the anus and insert his finger hoping to push out the stone from the bladder. (Kidney stones and gall stones were too far inside the body to be treated.)

Until the mid-19th century there were no **anaesthetics**. Patients might be given alcohol, or some form of opium from the poppy to help to ease the pain, but people were often fully conscious during an operation and could feel everything! Because operations were so painful and there were no anaesthetics, they needed to be carried out as quickly as possible and assistants were needed to keep the patient still. Complex operations that took a long time or went deep into the body were impossible and surgery tended to be seen as a last resort.

Source A: An amputation set from the 19th century.

Saw, to cut through the bone → ← Knives, to cut through skin, muscles, etc.

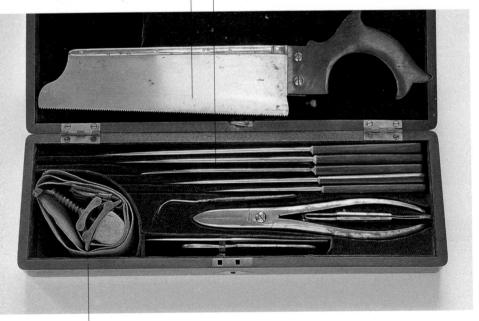

Screw **tourniquet** – the bandage was wrapped around the arm or leg and the screw was tightened so that the flow of blood was stopped while an amputation was being carried out

Source B: A picture of an amputation in the operating theatre of the old St Thomas' Hospital, London, around 1775.

Assistants holding the patient still

Everyone wearing ordinary clothes

Patient shouting

Spectators watching

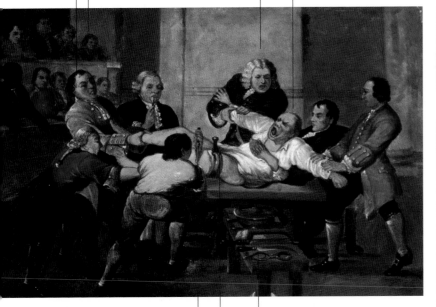

Sawdust on the floor to soak up the blood

Knives and saw laid out ready for use

Tourniquet around the thigh to stop the flow of blood to the leg

The following source describes the amputation of a leg at the hip joint.

Source C: From an account by Professor James Syme, who was Professor of Surgery at Edinburgh University from 1833 to 1869.

I inserted a narrow knife about a foot long. I cut along the bone, separating it from its socket. Finally I passed the knife around the top of the bone, cutting the remaining ligaments. This ended the operation which had not taken more than one minute.

My assistant slackened the tourniquet around the leg so that we could see how bad the bleeding was. It seemed at first sight as if there were so many blood vessels that they could never all be closed and we knew we must work quickly to prevent the patient's death.

Activities

1 Using Sources A, B and C, make a list of what the sources tell you about the way operations were carried out before anaesthetics were used.

2 Explain why people were so reluctant to have an operation in the early 19th century.

3 Why do you think surgeons did not perform operations on internal organs?

Summary

Operations in the 19th century were very painful and there were no anaesthetics available, so assistants were needed to hold the patient still and the surgeon needed to work quickly. Speed was also important because there was the danger of heavy blood loss, which could lead to death. The problem of infection meant that even if the patient survived the operation, they often died later.

5.2 The discovery of anaesthetics

Learning outcomes

By the end of this topic you should be able to:

- understand and explain the problems caused by the lack of anaesthetics
- explain the importance of the discovery of ether and chloroform

The discovery of an anaesthetic, which would reduce the pain felt by a patient, was a major breakthrough in surgery. It meant the surgeon could work more carefully and take more time if the patient was not struggling – although the problem of blood loss still meant that the surgeon could not take too long.

Date	Event
1799	Humphrey Davy accidentally discovered that inhaling nitrous oxide (also called laughing gas) made you less aware of pain.
1844–1845	Horace Wells, a dentist in the USA, used nitrous oxide when extracting teeth.
1846	William Morton, also a dentist in the USA, found that the gas ether was a more long-lasting anaesthetic. It was used in an operation to remove a growth from a patient's neck. In Britain, Robert Liston used ether while amputating a leg.

There was great excitement at the discovery of anaesthetics but there were also problems in the use of ether.

- It sometimes made patients vomit.
- It tended to irritate the lungs of patients so that they coughed even when they were unconscious.
- It was highly flammable, which was a dangerous situation when the only form of artificial light was from candles or gas lights.
- It tended to produce very deep sleep, which could last for days.
- It had to be carried in large, heavy glass bottles, which were very difficult for surgeons to carry around with them. (Remember many operations were still carried out in the patient's home.)

James Simpson and chloroform

A young surgeon in Edinburgh, James Simpson, wanted to discover a better anaesthetic than ether. One evening he invited some other doctors to his house, where they experimented by inhaling vapours from various chemicals. After Simpson's wife found them all unconscious, they realised that chloroform was extremely effective and it did not seem to have the negative side effects of ether.

Source A: A drawing made c1860 of Simpson and his friends, waking up after testing chloroform, in 1847.

Activity

1 Look at Source A. What do you think the artist is suggesting about the effects of chloroform?

2 What elements of the source have helped you to reach that understanding?

Simpson used chloroform in an operation in Edinburgh as early as 1847, but its use became far more widespread after he came to work in London and especially after Queen Victoria used chloroform during the birth of her eighth child in 1853. However, it was difficult to get the dose of chloroform correct – too little and the patient could still feel pain, but too much could be fatal, as was shown when Hannah Greener, a 14-year-old girl who was having an infected toenail removed, died almost immediately after being given the anaesthetic.

Chloroform affected the heart, and a number of young, physically fit patients died after inhaling it. However, in 1848, John Snow developed an inhaler that regulated the dosage and reduced the number of deaths.

Why did some people not want pain relief?

Not everyone welcomed the use of anaesthetics.

- The Victorians were very religious and some people felt that pain relief was interfering with God's plan, especially as the Bible said that God had told Eve that childbirth would be painful.
- Some people distrusted anaesthetics because they were new and their effects were not fully understood.
- Some doctors felt that it was easier for a patient to die if they had been made unconscious than if they remained awake and struggling.
- The number of patients who died shortly after their operations actually increased (see page 116) when anaesthetics were used, which seemed to prove that there was something wrong with anaesthetics.

The effects of both ether and chloroform tended to remain in the body for some time afterwards, so the search for a better anaesthetic continued. It was found that cocaine was effective for pain relief, but it was addictive. However, in 1884 it was discovered that cocaine could be used as a local anaesthetic – to numb a specific part of the body – instead of a general anaesthetic, which made the patient completely unconscious. In 1905 a more effective version, called novocaine, was developed to be used as a general anaesthetic.

> FASCINATING FACT
>
> In 1942, curare, a South American poison, was used as an anaesthetic. This didn't remain in the body for as long as ether or chloroform so patients recovered more quickly.

James Simpson was the first man to be knighted for services to medicine. When he died in 1870, over 30,000 mourners lined the streets of Edinburgh for his funeral. His family refused a burial in Westminster Abbey in London, but a plaque there is dedicated to him. It says 'To whose genius and benevolence, the world owes the blessings derived from the use of chloroform for the relief of suffering'.

Source B: Snow's chloroform inhaler, invented in 1848.

Activities

3 Why do you think James Simpson's discovery of chloroform is seen as an important advance in surgery when ether had already been discovered?

4 Explain the role of each of the following factors in the search for better anaesthetics:

   a) science and technology

   b) religion

   c) social attitudes.

5 Why did the discovery of anaesthetics still not solve the problem of the surgeon having to work quickly?

Summary

The discovery of an effective anaesthetic was a major breakthrough in surgery since it meant the patient was not in pain, and it was welcomed by many. However, some people were slow to accept the idea of anaesthetics, and there were drawbacks to the use of both ether and chloroform.

5.3 Source enquiry skills: inference

Learning outcomes

By the end of this topic you should be able to:

- demonstrate that a source can often provide more information than is stated or shown
- understand the way inferences can be made from sources
- make inferences from sources

Inference is the word used to describe something that you have worked out from a source, even though it is not actually stated or shown. The inference can be about the situation in the source or about the message that the author or artist wants to convey.

Small details can be very important. If you are looking at a picture source, for example a portrait or a cartoon, you need to think about:

- what details have been included
- what is the centre of attention (and how has the artist made it the centre of attention)
- whether people have been shown interacting with each other
- whether anything has been deliberately missed out.

The examination for Unit 3 will usually start with a question asking you what inferences you can make from a single source. This will often be phrased as 'What can you learn from Source X about...'. To do well, you must make sure that you explain which part of the source you have used to make each inference.

Look at Source C on page 109, Professor Syme's description of an amputation. He says that he used a knife that was about a foot long (30cm) – which suggests he needed to be able to cut deep into the hip joint. The inferences that the blood loss was very heavy and also that he knew that blood loss was a great problem in amputations are supported by his comment that they had to work quickly to close off the blood vessels that were bleeding in order to prevent the patient's death.

Look back to Source B (the picture of an amputation in 1775) on page 109. We can infer from this source that the patient is afraid and that operations were normally painful. The parts of Source B that support this inference are the fact that the patient is still conscious while on the operating table, which suggests he will feel pain. You can use details to show that the cartoonist has deliberately chosen to make the operation seem horrific. The patient is shown shouting and struggling and has to be held down by several people, which would suggest that he was afraid and in great pain.

Look back at Source A on page 110, the picture of Simpson and his friends. The artist has shown two of them asleep and one just waking up; two are on the floor and their chairs have been overturned. By showing them waking up after being unconscious and looking uncertain, we can infer that chloroform is a very strong and effective anaesthetic. We can also infer from the scene that Simpson is someone who is prepared to take risks and experiment on himself.

Activities

1 What can you infer from Source A below about the way operations were carried out in the early 19th century?

2 What can you infer from Source B below about Mantell's attitude towards the use of ether?

3 What can you infer from Source C below about people's attitudes towards Simpson and the discovery of anaesthetics?

Source A: A painting from 1817 showing an operation in a patient's home in Dublin to remove a tumour from a man's armpit.

Source B: From the diary of Gideon Mantell, a surgeon.

1 May 1847

Went to Bartholomew's Hospital and witnessed two operations under the influence of Ether: the first I have seen. The loss of feeling on both occasions was complete: the patient had no consciousness of the operation. But the effect on the patient afterwards was appalling, although brief.

Source C: A statue of James Simpson that was erected in Edinburgh after his death; the money for the statue came from collections from the public.

exam zone

Build better answers

What can you learn from Source A about the way operations were carried out in the early 19th century?   (6 marks)

■ **Basic, Level 1**
Answer describes the picture or explains how operations were carried out.

● **Good, Level 2**
Answer makes a comment about operations, but does not support it with details from the source.

▲ **Excellent, Level 3**
Answer takes details from the picture and links them to a range of comments about operations.

Summary

An inference is information that can be worked out (or 'learned') from a source even if it is not actually stated or shown in the details. In your answers you should make clear what it is that you have worked out and which part of the source has helped you to make that inference.

5.4 Source enquiry skills: purpose

Learning outcomes

By the end of this topic you should be able to:

- demonstrate an ability to analyse sources and show how an impression has been created
- use source analysis to understand what a source is showing or telling you
- use source analysis to identify purpose: why a source has shown or told you these things

When you analyse a source, you break it into sections and look at each part separately. You have seen that you need to analyse a source in order to make an inference about it. Identifying the purpose of a source works in the same way. You break down the different elements of a source and ask why the creator of the source has chosen to represent them in that way.

For example, Source D records the operation in 1846 when ether was used for the first time. The way the artist has chosen to represent the event deliberately creates the impression that it was an important event.

The extract from the Boston Daily Evening newspaper (Source A) describes the use of ether. As you read it, think about how we can tell that the writer of the article regards the use of ether as an amazing advance in surgery.

Source A: An extract from the *Boston Daily Evening* newspaper, 1 October 1846.

New and <u>Valuable</u> Discovery

We noticed yesterday the discovery of a new preparation by Dr Morton which is intended to reduce <u>the sufferings of those who are forced to undergo painful operations</u>. The effect of this new discovery is to make the patient unconscious and any <u>operation can then be performed without occasioning</u> pain. We are told by a gentleman of the highest respectability that he witnessed an experiment of the use of this <u>most extraordinary discovery</u> at the rooms of Dr Morton one evening this week. A painful tooth was extracted from the mouth of an individual <u>without giving him the slightest pain</u>. He was <u>put into a kind of sleep</u> by inhaling a portion of this preparation, the effects of which lasted for about three quarters of a minute, just long enough to extract the tooth. This discovery is destined to make a <u>great revolution</u> in the arts of surgery and surgical dentistry.

This report has chosen to highlight the benefits of ether in a way that most newspaper readers could relate to – contrasting the painful operations they were used to with operations 'without… pain'.

The use of language to indicate attitude, e.g. 'valuable', 'extraordinary discovery', 'great revolution' all show a positive view of discovery.

The report uses relatively simple language – 'put into a kind of sleep' – rather than medical terminology because it is written for a general readership.

Source B: From *The Scientific Revolution in Victorian Medicine* by A. J. Youngson, published in 1979.

Dragged unwillingly, or carried from the ward to the operating theatre by a couple of hospital attendants, the patient was laid on an operating table and, if necessary, strapped down, surrounded by curious strangers. The first cut of the scalpel must have caused searing pain and few patients were able to clench their teeth and remain silent. Shriek after shriek were more likely to fill the room, ebbing away to convulsive cries and sobs as the operation proceeded.

Source C: From a speech by James Simpson to a meeting of doctors in Edinburgh in 1847.

In years to come people will look back with sorrow at our reactions to anaesthetics. They will be amazed at the idea of humane men saying they prefer operating on patients who are conscious instead of anaesthetised, and that the fearful agonies of an operation should be endured quietly.

Source D: A painting showing Dr Morton's use of ether in an operation carried out by Dr Warren in 1846 in the USA.

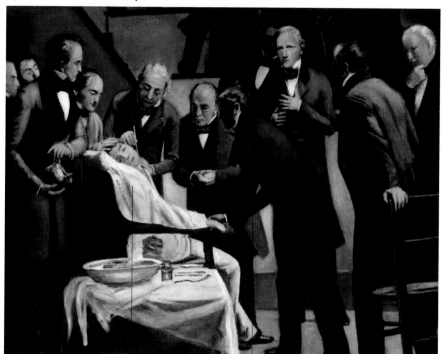

Portrayal of patient – the patient is shown completely relaxed, with a calm, passive expression.

Doctors are shown bending over in concern for the patient and fascination with the new technique.

Spectators are shown leaning in to see such an important event – the artist creates an atmosphere of rapt attention to a historic moment.

examzone

Build better answers

What was the purpose of this representation? Explain your answer, using source D and your own knowledge. (8 marks)

■ **Basic, Level 1**
Answer explains the purpose but doesn't say how the source shows this: e.g. *'To show how important the operation was.'*

● **Good, Level 2**
Answer explains the purpose and links this to details in the source: e.g. *'The painting shows doctors and spectators crowding round to see the operation, to show how important it was that ether was being used in an operation.'*

▲ **Excellent, Level 3**
Answer analyses the source to unpick its purpose. You will do best if you make clear use of your own relevant historical knowledge.

Activities

1 Study Source B. Use your source analysis skills to unpick the ways the author creates such a vivid description.

2 Source C shows Simpson making an argument against doctors who were doubtful about the benefits of anaesthetics.
   a) Why do you think some doctors preferred to operate on patients who were conscious?
   b) Why do you think Simpson wanted to make this speech?

Summary

You need to look at all the details in the source in order to work out what extra information can be squeezed from it. The details the author or artist has chosen to include can tell you a lot about the purpose of the source. Your own knowledge about the topic will also help you pin down its purpose.

6.1 Understanding infection

Learning outcomes

By the end of this topic you should be able to:

- explain the problem of infection
- understand why the problem of infection became worse after the use of anaesthetics
- understand the reasons why infection could not be dealt with in the mid-19th century

Antiseptic: Something that fights against sepsis and the microbes that create infection

Aseptic: Sterile; free from the microbes that cause infection

Sepsis: A condition in which harmful bacteria affect the flesh, normally leading to infection and decaying flesh

Source B: An example of gangrene.

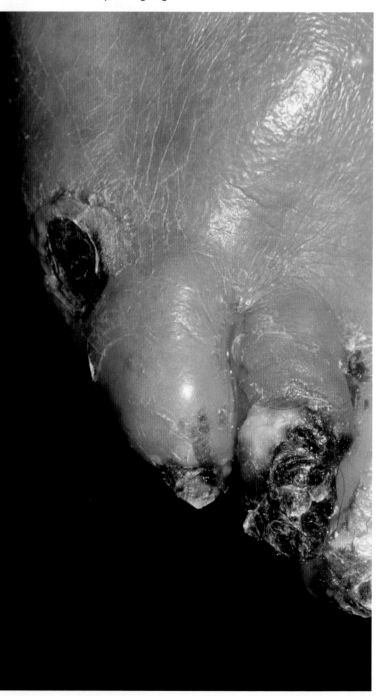

Source: A: From *Lord Lister, his life and work* by G. T. Wrench, 1913.

Getting rid of the dreadful pain which made an operation such a gruesome thing in the past, and which meant that only the most urgent operations were carried out, seemed to open out a new area for surgery. But in hospitals the new 'blessing' of anaesthetics also led to its own defeat. More operations were undertaken for smaller problems, and the dreadful problems of infection and gangrene swept through the wards with redoubled fury.

The problem of infection

The use of anaesthetics seemed to be a major breakthrough in surgery, but it created a new set of problems. As you have seen, when the patient was conscious, surgeons had to work quickly and could not do internal operations that would take a long time; but the use of anaesthetics meant that surgeons could take longer, and they began to do more complex operations. However, they did not understand about infection and germs, therefore many patients survived the operation but died a few days later from gangrene or **sepsis** – infection and decay that produced a strong smell of rotting flesh.

Operations were often carried out in the patient's home or the hospital ward but, even if they were done in an operating theatre, the conditions were not hygienic. Medical students would come to watch and there would be dressers (who held the patient down) all wearing their normal clothes. The surgeon would wear 'special' clothes – usually his oldest coat, with large amounts of dried blood and pus on it, which was seen as a sign that the surgeon was experienced. He might wash his hands in water but the instruments and the operating table would be dirty and unhygienic. Look back at Source B and read Source C on page 114 to remind yourself about the conditions in which operations were carried out. In these conditions it was not surprising that many patients died from infection.

There was still the problem of blood loss, which resulted in the death of many patients. All this meant that the number of deaths linked to surgery actually increased in the 1850s–1870s, and historians sometimes call this the 'Black Period' of surgery.

Early attempts to control infection

Ignaz Semmelweiss worked at Vienna General Hospital in Austria. In 1846 he was concerned that the death rate among women in childbirth was higher in the hospital, in the ward where medical students were involved, than in home births or in wards where midwives delivered the baby. The medical students often came straight from the dissecting room, where they were cutting dead bodies, to the childbirth delivery room. Semmelweiss found that making the students wash their hands using a chlorinated solution reduced the death rate dramatically.

Despite the change in the death rate, many other doctors made fun of Semmelweiss's ideas. He was sacked from the hospital and eventually left Vienna.

James Simpson copied Semmelweiss's ideas when he was Professor of Midwifery at Edinburgh University and, later, when he came to London. These methods were not widely accepted for some time.

Meanwhile Florence Nightingale set high standards of hygiene in her work in hospitals and the training of nurses – for example, she insisted on only one patient in each bed.

Source C: A ward at Netley Hospital in the late 19th century, showing the emphasis that was being placed on hygiene.

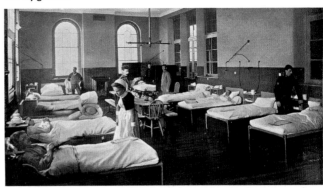

However, Nightingale did not actually understand how infection occurred. She believed in the miasma theory – that disease was caused by poisonous vapours. In fact, the idea of miasma and another idea – that oxygen in the air encouraged infection – led to wounds being tightly bandaged up, something that we now know keeps the temperature high and encourages the growth of bacteria. Consequently, the problem of infection in surgery had still not been solved.

Activities

1 Explain what Source A means when it says 'more operations were undertaken for smaller problems'.

2 Explain why the 1850s–1870s were called the 'Black Period' in surgery.

3 What can you infer from Source C about hygiene in this hospital ward?

4 Think about how operations were carried out and explain why Nightingale's emphasis on cleanliness and hygiene in the hospital wards would not have a big effect on the death rate after surgery.

Summary

Surgeons carried out a greater range of operations after the discovery of anaesthetics and they became more willing to carry our internal operations. However, because infection and microbes were not properly understood, the surgeon and his tools were likely to introduce infection into the wound and so the death rate from operations actually increased.

6.2 Joseph Lister and antiseptics

Learning outcomes

By the end of this topic you should be able to:

- show how Lister overcame the problem of infection
- demonstrate an understanding of how Lister's work led to progress in surgery
- understand the significance of Lister's work within the overall development of surgery

It was not until 1861 that the French chemist Louis Pasteur conducted experiments that proved that decay and infection were caused by microbes in the air. It took time for Pasteur's ideas to be accepted by scientists and even longer for the ideas to be applied to medicine and for surgeons to reach a proper understanding of infection.

Joseph Lister's use of carbolic acid

Joseph Lister was appointed Professor of Surgery at Glasgow University in 1859 and then became Surgeon at Glasgow Royal Infirmary in 1861. He was put in charge of a new building at the hospital. There was hope that the high death rate after operations could be reduced, but this did not happen. Between 1861 and 1865 half of the people who had operations died from infection.

> Lister tried various methods to encourage wounds to heal cleanly, without infection, but had little success.

> He became interested in Pasteur's work and especially the idea that microbes were responsible for infection in a wound.

> In 1864 he found that carbolic acid was used in the sewage works at Carlisle and that it killed parasites.

> Lister thought that carbolic acid could also be used to kill the microbes causing infection.

In 1865 he tested his ideas when an 11-year-old boy was brought into hospital with a compound fracture of his leg. In a compound fracture the bone pokes through the skin, creating an open wound; at this time infection would, almost inevitably, lead to death. Lister soaked the bandages in carbolic acid and watched the wound carefully – there was no sign of pus or infection and at the end of six weeks the fractured bone and the wound had healed.

Source A: Lister's own description of the treatment, from a letter to his father in 1866.

> Though I hardly expected any success I tried carbolic acid on the wound to prevent the formation of pus in the leg. Well it is now eight days since the accident and the patient has reacted just as if there had been no open wound.

Source B: A modern drawing showing Lister using carbolic spray in one of his earliest antiseptic surgical operations, c1871.

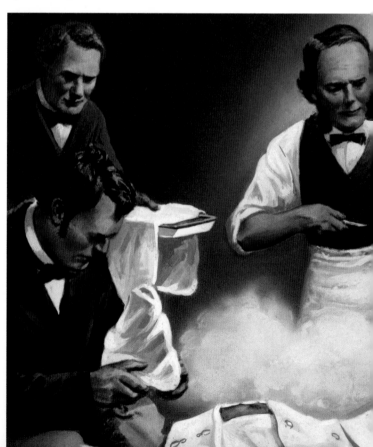

The spread of antiseptics

Lister now used a solution of carbolic acid to clean wounds, equipment and bandages, and in 1867 he announced that his wards had been free from sepsis for nine months. In 1877 he became Professor of Surgery at King's College Hospital in London and shortly afterwards carried out an operation on a kneecap under **antiseptic** conditions. This operation was widely publicised and other surgeons began to copy his methods.

> ### FASCINATING FACT
> Listerine was first produced in 1879 as a surgical antiseptic and was named in honour of Lister. In 1895 it was given to dentists for oral care and began to be sold to the public in the USA in 1914.

Lister's other achievements

At this time, silk was used as sutures (or stitches) to sew wounds closed, but there were two problems that caused infection.

- Silk did not absorb carbolic acid and therefore could not be sterilised.
- A thread had to be left dangling out of the wound so that the stitches could be pulled out once the wound had healed.

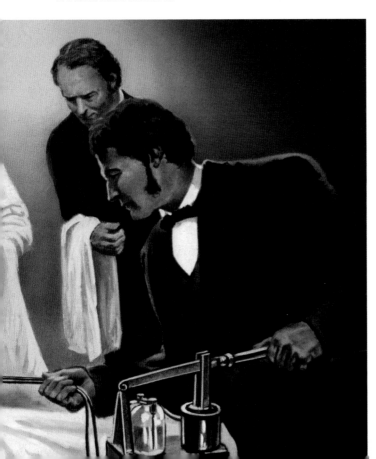

Source C: A photograph of an operation in the 1880s; the man on the right is operating a carbolic spray.

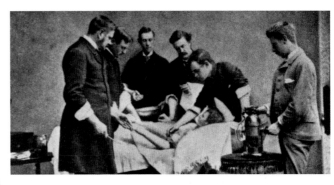

Lister introduced the use of catgut, which could be sterilised, and this reduced the chance of infection. He also developed a form of catgut that would dissolve after several days in the body, so there was no need to leave a thread dangling.

In recognition of the importance of all his work, Lister was given the title of baronet in 1883 and became Baron Lister in 1897. After Lister's death in 1912 a funeral service was held at Westminster Abbey and a fund was set up to organise lectures and statues in his honour. The Lister medal is the highest honour that can be given to a British surgeon.

Activities

1 Explain two ways in which Lister overcame the problem of infection.

2 Explain why Lister's work was such an important advance in surgery.

3 Explain the role of each of the following factors in Lister's development of antiseptics:

a) chemistry (especially the use of carbolic acid)

b) technology (especially the work needed to create a spray of carbolic acid during operations).

4 What evidence is there that the importance of Lister's work was recognised by both the medical profession and the public?

Summary

Lister's work in showing the importance of antiseptic conditions was an important breakthrough in surgery, although it took time to be fully accepted.

6.3 Reactions to Lister's antiseptics

Learning outcomes

By the end of this topic you should be able to:

- explain the various reasons why there was opposition to Lister's ideas
- understand the gradual shift from antiseptic to aseptic surgery

Although Lister's ideas were quickly accepted in Germany and the USA, many doctors in Britain were unconvinced at first and joked about 'Mr Lister's germs'. Meanwhile others accepted the basic idea of antiseptics but found the whole procedure too difficult or uncomfortable to put into practice especially as carbolic acid made the skin on their hands cracked and sore.

examzone
Watch out!

Some students assume that new discoveries were quickly accepted by everyone and that people who were slow to accept new ideas were stupid in some way. Many developments in surgery, such as the use of anaesthetics and antiseptics, were opposed at first and this opposition was based on a range of points, which included some valid ideas.

Opposition to Lister's ideas

There was a great deal of opposition to Lister.

- Some doctors didn't accept the idea that microbes caused infection because microbes could not be seen without a microscope.
- Using carbolic solutions slowed down the whole operation, which could lead to problems of blood loss.
- Doctors who copied Lister's ideas did not always copy them properly and then, if they did not get an improved survival rate after operations, they said that Lister's ideas were wrong.

- Lister himself kept changing his methods in an attempt to further improve his work – many doctors thought this meant he was not sure of his ideas.
- The equipment was expensive and heavy.
- Some surgeons had good results even without using carbolic acid.
- The nurses resented the extra work caused by this emphasis on hygiene.

However, in 1878 the German doctor Robert Koch identified the bacterium that causes blood poisoning and this helped to convince many people that Lister was right and that microbes do cause infection.

By 1890 most operations were carried out in antiseptic conditions and more complex procedures were undertaken. For example, in the 1880s an infected appendix was removed and in 1896 a surgeon repaired a heart that had been damaged by a stab wound.

Source A: From the memoirs of a doctor who worked with Lister.

Everything was soaked in carbolic – hands, instruments and the patients' skins. The whole scene of the operation was covered in its spray, which dispersed its globules into every nook and cranny of the wound. Our faces and coat sleeves often dripped with it. It was a relief to us all when the spray was [not used anymore]. It was costly and cumbersome and often broke down.

Activities

1 Classify the opposition to Lister under two headings: opposition based on scientific thinking; and opposition based on practical problems.

2 Compare Sources B and C. What are the main differences between antiseptic and aseptic conditions?

Source B: A modern operation in *aseptic* conditions.

Surgeons and nurses wearing operating gowns that can be sterilised

Surgeons and nurses wearing caps to keep hair tidy and prevent infection

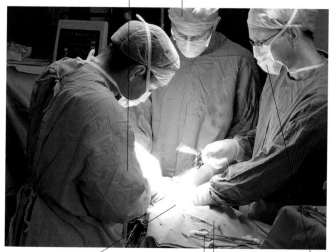

Surgeons and nurses wearing rubber gloves to prevent microbes from their hands getting into the wound or onto the equipment

All instruments sterilised

Sterile cloths to cover all other parts of the body and prevent infection

Surgeons and those close to the operation wearing masks to prevent themselves breathing infection into the wound

Source C: An operation in *antiseptic* conditions in 1900.

Nurses and surgeons wearing clean white aprons and shirts

Nurses wearing hats to keep hair tidy and prevent infection

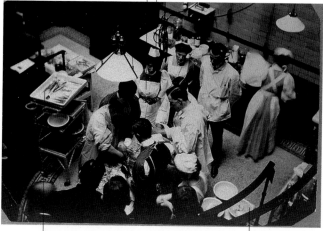

Instruments laid on a clean tray

Bowls so that dirty equipment can be moved away and cleaned afterwards

From antiseptic to aseptic

Robert Koch made another discovery in 1878: steam was more effective than carbolic acid at killing the microbes that cause infection. This meant everything that was used in an operation could be sterilised by using steam to kill all the microbes.

> **FASCINATING FACT**
>
> Nurse Caroline Hampton, who assisted the American doctor William Halstead, had severe eczema on her hands and carbolic acid was making it worse. In 1890 Dr Halstead asked Goodyear Rubber Company to make rubber gloves for her. A side effect of this was that scientists found out that wearing rubber or latex gloves helped to prevent bacteria being introduced into the wound by the surgeon's hands.

Developments such as the steam steriliser and rubber gloves were part of the shift from antiseptic methods (fighting infection and killing bacteria) to **aseptic** conditions, where doctors tried to prevent bacteria being anywhere near the wound. The use of masks, sterile equipment and closed operating theatres are all part of aseptic surgery (see Source B).

exam zone

Build better answers

Study Source C. What was the purpose of this representation? Explain your answer, using Source C and your own knowledge. (8 marks)

■ **Basic, Level 1**
Answer explains the purpose but doesn't say how the source shows this.

● **Good, Level 2**
Answer explains the purpose and links this to details in the source.

▲ **Excellent, Level 3**
Answer analyses the source to unpick its purpose. You will perform best if you make clear use of your own relevant historical knowledge.

Summary

Lister's use of carbolic acid as an antiseptic was an important breakthrough in surgery, and once the idea was accepted, the move was made towards aseptic conditions to prevent infection as far as possible.

6.4 Source enquiry skills: reliability

Learning outcomes

By the end of this topic you should be able to:

- understand that sources are not always completely reliable
- explain the factors affecting the reliability of a source
- evaluate the reliability of a source

Source A: A painting of Morton's 1846 operation by the artist Robert Hinckley.

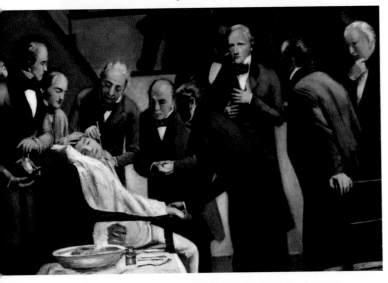

Source B: A photograph of Morton's 1846 operation.

In 1846 Morton used ether to anaesthetise a patient for Dr Warren, who then removed a growth from the patient's neck. Compare the painting of the operation, which you have already studied, to the photograph. The painting by Hinckley was completed in 1892 so you might question whether the artist saw the actual operation and how accurate his memory of it was. If he was not a witness, it would be helpful to know if he had seen the way operations were carried out, if he knew what the people involved looked like or whether the scene was totally made up. You might assume the photograph must be reliable – until you find out that the team assembled some time later for the photo to be taken, with someone else posing as the patient! There are clues to the fact that the photograph is posed, in the way that the people are grouped so that they can all be seen clearly. The fact that the patient was a different person shows that the photograph was intended to record the successful team, and it is those details that are most likely to be reliable. This shows how important it is to consider origins and intentions when you evaluate a source.

Before any source can be used, the historian always needs to evaluate its reliability by considering certain points. These will include the content and selection of the source, its origins, intentions and nature, as well as the language used.

An important thing to remember in your answer is to focus on the specific source. Newspapers may sometimes exaggerate and sensationalise their accounts in order to make them interesting and sell more copies – but this is not a relevant comment unless you can provide precise examples from the source to support your comment.

Look back to Source A on page 114. The writer of this article says ether is 'destined to make a great revolution', but his article gives a very factual description with little extreme language, and also emphasises that he got the information from someone of the 'highest respectability' who personally witnessed the use of ether. This newspaper account has not been sensationalised.

Biased sources

A source is likely to reflect the opinion of the author – not many people would bother to write about an event if they didn't have an opinion about it! But that doesn't mean the source is automatically unreliable. You need to decide if the writer's feelings are so strong and the account is so one-sided that the source cannot be trusted, in which case it is biased. Remember that if you say a source is biased you must always explain how that bias has affected the account (for example, whether it is biased in favour of Lister, giving him more credit than he deserves, or if it is biased against him, saying his achievement wasn't really important). You also have to be able to back up your comments with evidence of loaded language, exaggerations or factual inaccuracies.

Source C: From Knut Haeger, *An Illustrated History of Surgery*, published in 1988.

> Many of Lister's colleagues laughed at him, and Hughes Bennett, a professor of medicine at Edinburgh, asked scornfully 'Where are these little beasts? Show them to us and we shall believe in them. Has anyone seen them yet?' But Lister never bothered to reply and it is said that he only heaved an occasional sigh at the world's stupidity.

Hindsight and reliability

Source C was written with the benefit of hindsight. This means it was written after Lister and Pasteur had been proved correct, so the author could put the opposition to Lister in its historical context. But, in Source D, Lister certainly responds very strongly to criticism. Does that mean Source C is unreliable? Not necessarily, because Source D might be one exceptional case – the one time Lister did bother to reply to criticism – while Source C could be based on a much wider survey of all the criticism of Lister's approach, and all his responses (or lack of them) to this criticism.

Activities

1 Explain why each of the following is not automatically reliable:
- a photograph
- an eyewitness account.

2 Explain how an account written 100 years after an event, such as a historian's book, can still be a reliable source.

3 Study Source C. To what extent would you say that it is biased for or against Lister?

Source D: From an article by Lister in *The British Medical Journal* in February 1880, in which Lister responds to criticism.

> [Mr Spence] distinctly charges me with exaggeration, and hints that I give 'false facts'. This charge is a very serious one. I am not aware that I ever wrote anything that I did not believe to be strictly true… On what, then, is this grave charge founded? It is absolutely and utterly baseless; and I confess it fills me with astonishment…

examzone
Build better answers

How reliable are Sources C and D as evidence of Lister's response to criticism of his antiseptic system? Explain your answer, using Sources C and D and your own knowledge. (10 marks)

 Basic, Level 1
Answer gives a simple measure of reliability based on the nature of the sources: e.g. how much detail they go into or when each was written.

 Good, Level 2
There are two approaches: 1) answer looks at how reliable the information in the sources is, by comparing them and comparing with own knowledge; 2) answer focuses on the authorship of the sources and whether it is reliable, authoritative, representative.

▲ **Excellent, Level 3**
Answers at this level combine both the approaches in Level 2, using own knowledge of the historical context.

Summary

A source's reliability is affected by a range of factors but few sources are totally reliable or unreliable. You need to decide *how far* a source is reliable and show how you reached your judgement, using both the source and your own knowledge.

7.1 The problem of blood loss

Learning outcomes

By the end of this topic you should be able to:

- understand the problems of blood loss and 'shock'
- identify the problems with 19th century blood transfusion attempts
- explain the importance of Landsteiner's work in establishing blood types

Cautery: The use of heat to seal blood vessels and stop bleeding

Ligature: A thread tied around a blood vessel to stop bleeding

Shock: When there isn't enough blood in the circulatory system to keep the body working properly

Transfusion: The process of giving blood from a donor to the patient

Blood loss has always been a major problem in surgery. Bleeding makes it difficult for the surgeon to see what he is doing, but there is also the problem of '**shock**': if a patient loses too much blood, their body cannot function and they will die.

Medical descriptions of shock were not made until the 18th century, which is surprising considering the amount of blood lost in human history! This was probably in part because of the deeply-held medical belief that bleeding people was an effective treatment for many kinds of disorders – including the symptoms of shock, which were confusion, rapid breathing and a fast pulse.

During the 17th century, there were experiments with blood **transfusions** using blood from animals (usually sheep) as well as from humans. Although patients occasionally survived, in most cases they died and the procedure was banned.

Once anaesthetics and antiseptics made it possible to perform complex operations, there was a renewed drive to find a way of dealing with the two problems of blood loss: controlling blood loss and replacing lost blood.

Controlling blood loss

The usual way to deal with wounds or amputations was to seal the blood vessels by placing a hot iron onto the wound or pouring hot oil over it. This process was called **cautery** and was extremely painful.

In the 16th century a French surgeon, Ambroise Paré, developed metal clips to place on arteries during an operation. He also tried using silk thread to tie the blood vessels after an amputation instead of using heat to seal them. This was far less painful, but the **ligatures** did not always stop the bleeding if they were not tied properly.

Furthermore, this was before Pasteur developed the germ theory and therefore there was no understanding of the way that a surgeon's dirty hands inside a wound increased the chances of infection and led to a higher death rate. For these reasons, cautery continued to be the main way of dealing with bleeding until Paré's idea of silk ligatures was further developed by Joseph Lister in the late 19th century (see page 119).

Source A: A description of surgery in the 1840s by Dr Abbot. This describes an operation in the US but the same procedure would have taken place in Britain.

I remember an operation upon a young man for the removal of a large cancerous growth on the end of his tongue. The operation was done by a short, quick stroke of a knife which removed the outer half of the tongue. Of course, the bleeding was quite free. Dr Warren stepped back to the furnace where the hot iron was. At a look from Dr Warren the assistant quickly slipped both of his hands over the patient's eyes and the hot iron was instantly applied to the whole bleeding surface of the tongue. The patient jerked suddenly backwards. Driven almost insane by the pain and the sizzle of his searing flesh, the patient broke free from his restraint, and a bloody struggle ensued with the attendants who attempted to hold him down.

The problems with transfusion

In the 19th century a doctor called James Blundell brought blood transfusions back into medical practice in Britain. His speciality was the care of women during pregnancy and birth. The most common cause of death during childbirth was a massive amount of blood loss right after the baby was born. Blundell found that a transfusion of human blood could sometimes stop the mother from dying.

Spurred on by this, Blundell and his followers developed different kinds of syringes, pumps and tubes to help make their transfusions. But there were three main problems:

- Clotting – just as a scab forms over a wound, blood starts to clot as soon as it leaves the body. Blood clots in the transfusion tubes would block them up so the transfusion couldn't continue.
- Availability – clotting also meant that blood couldn't be stored. Transfusions could only be done with the donor (the person giving the blood) attached to the recipient (the person getting the blood), as shown in Source B.
- Immune response – experience had shown that transfusing blood from an animal into a human seemed to destroy human blood cells, often leading to death. A similar reaction seemed to happen with some human blood: the donor blood would cause the recipient's red blood cells to clump together. We now know that this happens because of an immune system response: antibodies don't recognise the donor blood and attack it.

Source B: A drawing of a 19th-century blood transfusion.

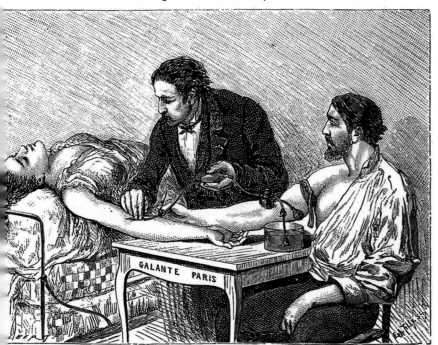

Blood types

The problem of the immune response was solved in 1901 when Karl Landsteiner suggested that there were different blood types – A, B and O. A fourth group, AB, was added in 1902 by two other scientists.

Landsteiner's findings showed that some of the blood types were incompatible – they could not be mixed without potentially fatal consequences. But transfusions between people of the same blood type were safe.

However, even with this breakthrough, the number of transfusions didn't increase very much. There was still the problem that a donor needed to be present to provide the blood whenever it was needed. This was not very practical and therefore Landsteiner's work did not have a big immediate effect on surgery.

Activities

1. Use details from Source B to describe the way in which transfusions were carried out in the 19th century.

2. Explain why 19th century surgeons had success with some transfusions but continued to experience major problems with others.

3. Landsteiner's work solved a major problem of blood transfusion. Why do you think it did not immediately make much impact on the number of transfusions carried out?

Summary

By the 19th century, methods to control blood loss had become very sophisticated. Although the 19th century saw blood transfusion reintroduced into medicine, there were too many problems with it for it to become widespread practice.

7.2 Dealing with blood loss

> ### Learning outcomes
>
> By the end of this topic you should be able to:
>
> - understand the development of transfusion and blood storage techniques
> - identify the key stages in dealing with the problem of blood loss
> - evaluate the role played by war, science and technology in overcoming the problem of blood loss

Transfusion and the First World War

James Blundell, the surgeon who reintroduced blood transfusion in the 19th century, wrote that cases 'really requiring the infusion of blood into the veins are probably rare'. That was in 1828. The First World War (1914-1918) changed everything. The industrial scale of the war led to millions of casualties. Many soldiers were dying from blood loss even when the wound itself was not fatal. Their bodies lost too much blood to be able to function: they went into shock and died.

Source A: A newspaper illustration from between 1914 and 1919 showing soldiers wounded in the First World War coming back to London by train for treatment.

Although transfusions were much less risky now that compatible blood groups had been identified, the problem of blood clotting meant that the donor had to be connected to the recipient. This was impossible to organise on the scale it was needed in wartime. Some way of storing blood was desperately required.

Storing blood

- In 1915 an American doctor, Richard Lewisohn, found that adding sodium citrate stopped blood from clotting. This meant that the donor did not have to be present and therefore more transfusions could be carried out. Although it was found that the blood cells would deteriorate if the blood was not used soon afterwards, this discovery still saved the lives of thousands of wounded soldiers.
- Richard Weil found that this blood could then be stored in refrigerated conditions.
- In 1916 Francis Rous and James Turner found that adding a citrate glucose solution allowed blood to be stored for longer. This meant that, when an attack was planned, the army could ask for donations of blood from the public, so that they were available for transfusion to treat the wounded.
- Geoffrey Keynes, a British surgeon, developed a portable machine that could store blood. This meant that transfusions could happen closer to the battlefield.
- The first blood depot was established in 1917 for the Battle of Cambrai, using blood group O, which can be safely given to all patients, whatever their blood type.

All these techniques were developed to get blood into wounded soldiers quickly and easily, so they would survive long enough to get to a field hospital where they could be patched up. There was no problem with donors for blood as soldiers were always ready to help wounded comrades.

Transfusion after the First World War

After the war finished, however, many British surgeons were not convinced that using stored blood for transfusions was as good a method as the old, direct method, with the donor connected directly to the recipient.

- Blood groups sometimes got confused: there were different classification systems and mix-ups produced unfortunate results.
- The bottles that blood was stored in and the transfusion tubes weren't always free of bacteria. This could cause infections after transfusions.
- Type O worked for everyone but that meant hospitals only targeted type O people for donations. As giving blood also involved a big cut into the vein, it quickly became difficult to find donors.
- Doctors and surgeons were simply reluctant to change – methods developed in haste to cope with the bloodbath of the First World War seemed risky.

Activities

1 Explain why it wasn't possible to use direct transfusion (connecting a donor to a recipient) to treat all the men needing blood transfusions in the First World War.

2 Explain which was more important in the development of blood transfusions – Landsteiner's identification of blood groups or Rous and Turner's discovery of ways to store blood.

3 Explain which factor had more effect on the development of blood transfusions – science and technology or war.

FASCINATING FACT

A Soviet scientist, Alexander Bogdanov, believed that regular transfusions of new blood could have major health benefits. He died after having a transfusion of blood from a student with malaria.

 examzone

Build better answers

Why were there problems with using 19th century methods of blood transfusion in the First World War? Explain your answer, using Source B on page 125 and your own knowledge. (10 marks)

■ **Basic, Level 1**
Answer uses simple statements from the source or own knowledge, e.g. *'There were too many soldiers needing transfusions.'*

● **Good, Level 2**
Answer is supported by information from the source or own knowledge, e.g. *'Source B shows that 19th century blood transfusions needed the donor to be connected to the patient. In the First World War, it was difficult to find the right donor at the right time and place.'*

▲ **Excellent, Level 3**
Answer uses the source and precise own knowledge. Answers must also use own knowledge.

Summary

Overcoming the problem of blood loss was an important stage in the development of surgery. It depended on increased scientific knowledge but its development was also accelerated by the casualties of war – though, as we have seen in other developments, this increased focus diminished as the war ended and old methods reasserted themselves.

7.3 Source enquiry skills: source comprehension in context

Learning outcomes

By the end of this topic you should be able to:

- select relevant details from a source
- identify the context of a question
- use details from a source to support an argument

Causation and context

When an exam question asks you to 'explain why…', it is a question about causation – why something happened (or didn't happen). However, you can't just make up your own reason. Your explanation has to show you know about the historical context.

Context means an understanding of the topic that the question sits in. If an exam question was a dumpling, the context would be the stew in which the dumpling was sitting.

So, as soon as a question includes the word 'Lister', for example, your brain should be thinking about the context of that topic.
For example:

Pre-Lister

- Discovery of anaesthetics
- Problem of infection
- Black Period of surgery

Lister and sutures

- Developed form of catgut to be used as sutures (stitches) – dissolved in body

Lister

Lister and carbolic acid

- Pasteur + germ theory
- High death rate at Glasgow Royal Infirmary
- 1865 – Lister experiments with carbolic acid: success
- 1870s onwards – other surgeons start to copy Lister's success

Opposition to Lister

- Opposition to germ theory
- Practical problems with carbolic solutions
- Some problems replicating results
- Lister kept changing his methods

The question will identify what aspect about Lister it is that you need to focus on. For example: 'Explain why there was opposition to Lister's ideas' would mean your focus should narrow to what you know about opposition to Lister.

'Explain why…' exam questions come with a source for you to use with your answer. Have a quick skim through the source, but it's a good idea to note down what you know about the subject of the question. Then have a look at the source and think about what it shows.

You then need to bring together what you know about the topic with the detail from the source. There will be relevant details in the source that you can use in your answer.

The rest of the explanation needs to come from you. This additional knowledge that you provide is what will lift your answer to the very top of the mark scheme.

Useful information

There are very few things that everyone agrees on completely in history. Historians put forward interpretations of different sources. That is to say, they make a case about what caused something to happen in the past. Other historians might interpret a source in a different way and put forward a different interpretation.

Source comprehension is about understanding what information a source is giving you and which bits are relevant to the question you have been asked. Once you have unpicked that information, you can put it together with your own knowledge to provide your own explanation of the exam question.

The key point here is that you are only interested in how the source can help you answer the question: which details are relevant to the question and which are not.

For example, here's a question 3-style question:

> Why was Lister's work such an important advance for surgery? Explain your answer, using Source A and your own knowledge.

Source A: A table based on Lister's own records, showing the death rate among amputation cases before and after the use of carbolic acid.

Years	Total cases	Survived	Died	Death rate
1864 to 1866	35	19	16	46%
1867 to 1870	40	34	6	15%

This source is very useful proof of the importance of Lister's work. The most useful detail is that death rates from amputations were reduced from 46 per cent before Lister started using antiseptic methods to 15 per cent after he started using them.

The table also provides information on which years he started using carbolic acid, and how many cases of amputations were involved, but these are not as directly relevant to the question.

Here's the same question again, this time with a different source:

> Why was Lister's work such an important advance for surgery? Explain your answer, using Source B and your own knowledge.

Source B: Publicity 'blurb' for a book called *Joseph Lister and the Story of Antiseptics* by John Bankston.

> None of the doctors could figure it out. During the nineteenth century, surviving surgery was only half the battle. In many hospitals, 50 percent of amputees lived through their painful operations only to die soon afterwards in their beds. Everyone had a theory for what doctors referred to as 'hospitalism'. But it was not until Joseph Lister and his pioneering work in antiseptic methods that death rates were greatly reduced after surgery. His work is so important that surgical history is divided into two eras: Before Lister and After Lister.

This source has some valuable information that is directly relevant to the question. For example, doctors were puzzled by the high death rate for amputees who had survived their operations, and this death rate was reduced after Lister introduced antiseptic techniques.

Would the statement about the periods 'Before Lister and After Lister' be relevant? It is not as useful for answering the question. The question already says that Lister's work was important. This statement just repeats that information without helping you explain why.

Activities

Provide the historical context for these three questions:

Why was blood transfusion so often unsuccessful in the 19th century?

Why did improvements in anaesthetics lead to the 'Black Period' of surgery?

Why was James Simpson's work important?

Summary

It is the question you are asked that makes source details relevant or not. Knowledge of historical context should set off your explanation on a specific route and you should only take what you need from a source to help you on your route.

8.1 The role of war in the development of surgery c1845–c1918

Learning outcomes

By the end of this topic you should be able to:

- explain the link between war and developments in surgery
- show an understanding of the role played by war in the development of surgery
- evaluate the role played by war in the development of surgery

Plastic surgery: Surgery carried out in order to change the appearance of the patient

Prosthetic limb: Artificial arm or leg, often made from metal and plastic

In this section, you need to look back at the role of various factors and consider what effect they had on developments in surgery – did they make a development possible, speed it up or hold it back?

War

Source A: A field surgery basket containing equipment for surgery to be carried out during a battle in the First World War.

In the First World War (1914–1918), surgeons often treated wounded soldiers close to the front line of fighting where the difficult conditions and large numbers of injuries put them under immense pressure. Surgeons therefore gained a great deal of experience in a wide range of injuries and sometimes had to improvise new techniques. In this way, war can be said to have accelerated their training.

Source B: A painting by Henry Tonks, a surgeon and artist, showing a military dressing station in France in 1918. A dressing station was the place where the injured would receive basic treatment before they were sent to hospital for more complicated treatment.

New developments in surgery

- The use of explosive weapons meant that many soldiers suffered deep wounds, and when fragments of clothing (or shrapnel) entered the wound, it caused infection. Surgeons found that cutting away infected tissue and soaking the wound with a saline (salt) solution was the best way of dealing with this.
- Before the First World War, most surgeons stayed away from working on the brain – it was far too complicated and risky. But the huge numbers of brain injuries in the war meant surgeons had to try something. For example, surgeons used rubber bands around patients' heads to control bleeding, saline solution to wash out pulped brain and even experimented with using magnets to pull metal fragments out of brain tissue.
- At the start of the First World War, the New Zealand doctor Harold Gillies asked for permission to set up a **plastic surgery** unit in the British army.

The development of plastic surgery

Before First World War French surgeon Morestin worked on facial surgery.	→	Gillies was aware of these developments and asked for permission to set up a plastic surgery unit in the British army.	→	Gillies began to experiment with ways of reconstructing facial injuries and paid particular attention to the attempt to create a normal appearance.
Before First World War French and German surgeons were developing skin graft techniques, using tissue from another part of the body to repair an injury.				

He kept careful records, including drawings of the injuries and the reconstructions he created.

He developed the new technique of pedicle tubes.
- A narrow layer of skin was lifted up from the body and stitched into a tube at one end.
- The other end was still attached to the body and this meant blood continued to circulate and helped healthy skin to develop.
- When the tube had grown long enough, the free end was attached to the new site.
- Once the skin graft was in place, the pedicle tube could be cut free at the base.

Source C: A photograph of a patient undergoing plastic surgery, showing pedicle tubes being used to graft skin onto the face.

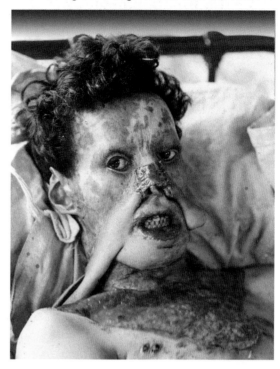

Prosthetic limbs

Between 1914 and 1921 over 41,000 men in the British armed forces lost a limb. Advances in **prosthetic limbs** included the use of light metal alloys and new mechanisms, but there were long waiting lists for these to be fitted and patients then needed training to use them properly.

Summary

War had a big effect on surgery and led to much progress being made, especially in brain surgery and plastic surgery. However, it also had the effect of focusing attention on dealing with wounds, and so progress in other areas of surgery, such as the search for better anaesthetics, may have been delayed as a result.

Activities

1 Draw a topic web summarising the different ways in which war affected developments in surgery.

2 Give one example of each of the following:
   a) war accelerating developments in surgery
   b) war leading to new developments in surgery.

8.2 The role of science and technology in the development of surgery c1845–c1918

Science

Chemistry played an important part in developing anaesthetics and antiseptics. These developments then made surgeons willing to try more complex operations, for example removing tumours. They also began to deal with internal obstructions, such as the hard 'stones' inside the gall bladder formed from cholesterol or pigments from blood cells (an extremely painful condition). In the 1880s operations to remove gallstones and the gall bladder became routine as a result of better anaesthetics and antiseptics. This also led to other procedures being developed to deal with internal problems, for example, the removal of the appendix. Chemistry was also important in the development of a suitable technique to store blood until it was needed for transfusion.

> **FASCINATING FACT**
> In 1902 Edward VII was diagnosed with appendicitis. He wanted to delay the operation to remove his appendix because he was due to be crowned at Westminster Abbey the next day but Lister told him, 'In that case, Your Majesty, it will be a corpse that is crowned.'

Infection was controlled by using Lister's carbolic spray, sterilising the instruments, wearing rubber gloves and using sterilised catgut for ligatures. In the move to aseptic surgery, gowns and face masks were also used and the operating theatre was a closed environment. This was all based on Pasteur's work on the germ theory, an understanding of chemistry and biology, and the development of the new science, bacteriology.

Source A: A steam steriliser, which could be used to sterilise surgical instruments.

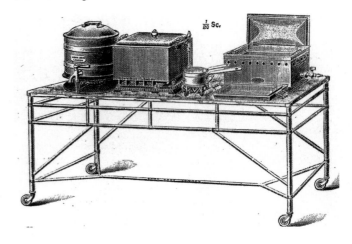

The discovery of X-rays by Wilhelm Roentgen in 1895 made surgeons more confident about internal operations. Roentgen did not take out a patent on his discovery, which meant people were free to copy his ideas. As a result, the use of X-rays spread very quickly – the London Royal Hospital had its first X-ray machine in 1896. X-rays also made it possible for surgeons to extract bullets and shrapnel without having to dig around in a wound, and this reduced the problems of bleeding and infection. The importance was quickly recognised by surgeons, and mobile X-ray units were developed for use during the First World War for the benefit of surgeons working in the front line.

Source B: A modern X-ray showing the chest of someone affected by shrapnel after a bomb blast.

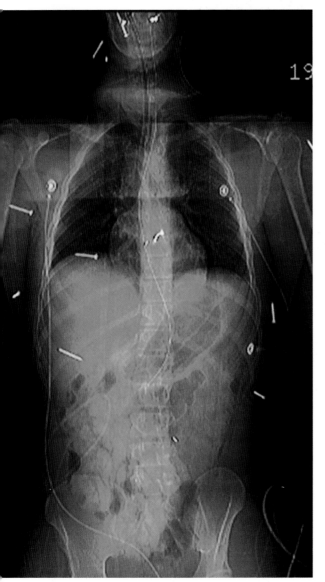

Technology

Developments in surgery are closely linked to improvements in scientific knowledge, for example discoveries about germs, anatomy, X-rays and chemicals. However, the role of technology is also very important. When chloroform was first administered, it was usually done by pouring some drops onto a handkerchief for the patient to inhale. As you have seen, it was difficult to get the dosage right and chloroform affected the heart, leading to the death of some patients. Dr John Snow's chloroform inhaler (see page 111) was much safer.

Other important examples of technology helping surgery to advance are the carbolic spray, the steam steriliser, the X-ray machine and the hypodermic needle (invented in 1853 by Alexander Wood) used in blood transfusions.

Source C: A diagram of a late 19th-century hypodermic needle.

Activity

Look at these examples of science and technology linked to surgery. Explain why science by itself would not have had much effect on surgery.

Science	Technology
Improved understanding of anatomy and physiology helped surgeons when they began to do more complex operations.	X-rays were discovered by Wilhelm Roentgen in 1895 and X-ray machines were installed at many hospitals within 10 years.
Experiments were undertaken to find the most effective anaesthetic.	Equipment was developed to deliver anaesthetics and then to measure the dose.
Pasteur's germ theory showed how microbes spread infection.	Carbolic spray, steam sterilised instruments and sterilised catgut all helped to cut down on infection in surgery.
Knowledge of chemistry helped to develop techniques for storing blood to use in transfusions.	The invention of the hypodermic needle in 1853 by Alexander Wood made it possible to measure an injection of a drug or a withdrawal of blood.

Summary

Science played an important role in suggesting ways of improving surgery, but technology was needed to put these ideas into practice.

8.3 Communications and the development of surgery

Learning outcomes

By the end of this topic you should be able to:

- explain the role of communications in the development of surgery
- demonstrate the interaction of different factors in the development of surgery
- evaluate the importance of various factors in the development of surgery

The spread of ideas: journals

The development of surgery depended on the effective communication of findings, evidence and techniques. If other surgeons never heard about new methods, then they would not spread. More than that, other surgeons had to be convinced that new methods were worth trying.

Reports of new discoveries in medical journals, such as the one produced by the Royal College of Surgeons, were very important in the communication of ideas between surgeons because:

- most surgeons read the same journals
- journals only published information that they thought was based on good science.

For example, Pasteur published his germ theory that microbes in the air caused decay and infection, and Lister applied this idea to his attempts to reduce infection. In this way, Lister was able to build on Pasteur's work and communication helped surgery to advance.

Source A From a letter from Lister to Pasteur in February 1874.

> ...your brilliant researches, proved to me the truth of the germ theory. You furnished me with the principle upon which alone the antiseptic system can be carried out.

Overcoming obstacles

Medical journals also communicated problems with new techniques and criticisms of new ideas. For example, the death of Hannah Greener from chloroform was reported in the medical journal *The Lancet*.

So the spread of ideas was not an automatic process. As you have seen, many new ideas were initially rejected or only accepted gradually. A lot depended on the individual too, and the context in which their work was communicated.

Someone else might have discovered how to use carbolic acid instead of Lister, but the fact that he kept careful records, publicised his ideas, tried different methods and was prepared to keep on with his ideas even when he was ridiculed all helped to get his ideas accepted.

Remember that when Semmelweiss tried to improve hygiene, he was unsuccessful. Lister's ideas were accepted more readily than Semmelweiss's because Pasteur had published his germ theory – but, even so, Lister's ideas were accepted in Germany and the USA before they were widely accepted in Britain.

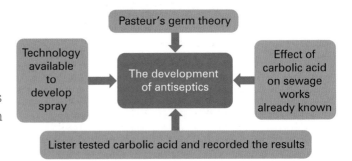

Inevitable progress?

Some of the developments you have studied would probably have happened anyway. The use of ether had been such a breakthrough in surgery that, when people realised the problems involved in using it, they did not want to abandon anaesthetics – they just wanted to find a better one.

Simpson set out to discover a new anaesthetic, but if he had not discovered chloroform, someone else probably would have done. However, the fact that Queen Victoria's doctor was a friend of Simpson perhaps led to its use on royalty, which then convinced many other people that it was an example of progress.

Communication breakdowns

Nevertheless, communication was not always effective. Lister did not know about the work of Semmelweiss, and Morestin was unwilling to share his ideas on plastic surgery with Harold Gillies. The spread of new ideas was sometimes restricted when people protected their new ideas from being copied by other people with patents.

The reason why surgeons were able to make use of X-rays so soon after Roentgen's discovery was because he published his work and did not take out a patent to prevent other people from copying his ideas. This was an unusual and remarkable decision considering how much money he could have made from his discovery.

The spread of ideas: newspapers and public opinion

The public were also interested in developments in surgery. For example, newspapers reported the first use of anaesthetics, Queen Victoria's use of chloroform and the removal of King Edward VII's appendix. These make very useful and interesting sources for historians, but public opinion was also important at the time as an influence on the development of surgery.

For example, during the 19th century many surgeons were troubled by the idea of using anaesthetics to make childbirth less painful. This was because the Bible said God had made childbirth painful for all women as a punishment for what Eve had done in the Garden of Eden.

When John Snow gave Queen Victoria chloroform for the delivery of her eighth child, *The Lancet* was very critical. But Prince Albert, Queen Victoria's husband, did not want her to suffer such pain if she did not have to. Many other influential husbands (and their wives) thought the same.

Growing public support meant that anaesthetics were soon widely used in childbirth.

Source B: An extract from the *Chester Chronicle* newspaper, 18 April, 1857.

The bulletins issued by the royal physicians from Buckingham Palace announce that the Queen and the infant princess are going on favourably [which] is in a great manner owing to the admirable manner in which chloroform was administered to her Majesty by Dr. Snow. The pains of labour came on on Tuesday morning about half-past three o'clock; and in the course of the morning it was thought advisable to administer chloroform, which was accordingly done by Dr. Snow, who kept her Majesty under its influence, with a few short intermissions, for three hours.

Activities

1. Explain how good communications have affected progress within surgery and acceptance of new ideas by the public.

2. Draw a picture to show the factors and events involved in the development of (a) aseptic surgery and (b) blood transfusions. You could use the image of a relay race, or a team climbing up a cliff face to show how early developments contributed to later discoveries.

3. How important do you think individuals were in these developments? For example, was so much work being done on anaesthetics that chloroform would have been discovered anyway? Lister was Professor of Surgery at Glasgow University – if carbolic acid had been discovered by someone else, would they have been in a position to publicise it so much?

Summary

Various factors were involved in developments in surgery, often interacting with each other, so that war, science, technology and communications all contributed to developments such as blood transfusions and anaesthetics.

8.4 Source enquiry skills: reaching a judgement

136

Learning outcomes

By the end of this topic you should be able to:

- understand the need to consider several aspects of an issue
- analyse the questions and plan a suitable response

The final question in the examination will always require you to use sources and your own knowledge to make a judgement about an interpretation of history. It will ask you how far you agree with a statement about surgery in this period. You should also remember that in history there is rarely a clear-cut answer – usually you have to weigh up two sides of an issue.

It is important to plan your answer so that you build up a logical argument rather than produce random comments. You also need to make sure that your comments are all supported by points from the sources in the examination paper and from your own knowledge. Study the following example.

Source A suggests that the communication of scientific knowledge was the most important factor in the development of antiseptics. How far do you agree with this interpretation? Explain your answer using your own knowledge, Sources A, B and C, and any other sources you find helpful.

Start by analysing the question.

- What topic knowledge do you need?
  Facts about antiseptics and Lister.
- What does the question want you to do?
  Explain the factors involved in why antiseptics developed and show which was the most important.
- How do you do it?
  Show the effect of each factor on the development of antiseptics and make a judgement about their importance.

Look at the sources, how can you use them to support your comments?

Source A: From a letter from Lister to Pasteur, February 1874.

I give you thanks for having, by your brilliant researches, proved to me the truth of the germ theory. You furnished me with the principle upon which alone the antiseptic system can be carried out.

Lister is clearly saying that Pasteur's work on the germ theory was the basis for his work on antiseptic techniques.

This suggests communication of scientific knowledge was the key factor.

Source B: From a letter written by Lister to his family shortly after he began at King's College Hospital, London.

The theatre was again well filled and I felt very nervous before the operation, yet I lost all consciousness of the presence of the spectators once I started the operation. Just before I began I remembered that only one Spectator mattered [God] and this thought gave me increased firmness.

The presence of spectators shows Lister is publicising his new technique, hoping that students will use it in their work.

Lister's comments suggest that he was a determined individual and gives an insight into Lister's beliefs and how he is strengthened by his religion to stay focused on surgery.

 **examzone** Watch out!

The question will always tell you to use the sources and your own knowledge. Beware of only using the sources and not adding in comments from your own knowledge. You need to refer to the sources and your own knowledge.

Source C: An illustration from W. Cheyne's book, *Antiseptic Surgery*, published in 1882. The caption gave the instruction: 'The surgeon should always have his hands in the spray and the assistant hands the instruments into the spray.'

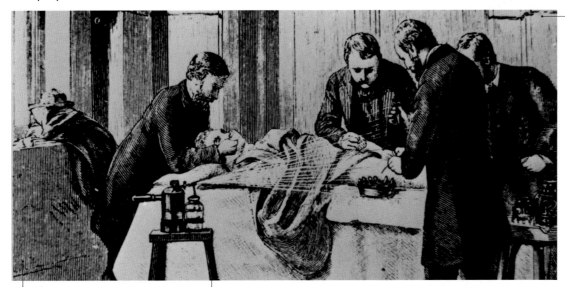

The publication of this book shows the importance of communication in spreading ideas (and Source A shows the importance of Pasteur's work being communicated to Lister).

The book tells other surgeons how to use the carbolic spray.

This shows the importance of technology in making the spray.

Now think about your own knowledge. What can you add about how Lister developed carbolic acid as an antiseptic?

Plan your answer.

- We have identified four factors here – science, the individual, technology and communications. You need to explain the role played by each of these in the development of antiseptics.
- When historians try to explain why something happened, they usually talk about a web of causation in which several factors interact, rather than a single chain of events with one thing leading directly to another. You could do a quick diagram to show how the factors involved in the development of antiseptics interacted.

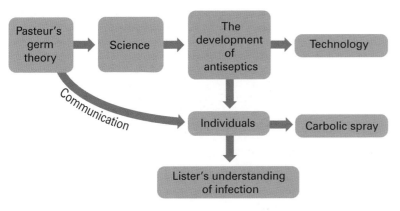

- The question asks how far you agree that the communication of scientific knowledge was the main factor, so in your answer you should try to weigh up each separate factor – was any one factor so important that antiseptics would not have been developed without it?
- Organise your answer so that it considers the evidence that backs up the interpretation and then the evidence that does not support it or which supports a different point of view. End with a balanced judgement to show how far you agree with the interpretation.
- Question 5 in the exam paper will have three marks available for spelling, punctuation and grammar (SPaG). While it is important to write clearly and correctly in all your answers so your answer is easy to understand, take particular care with question 5. Using specialist terms correctly is important here too.

Summary

Different people could reach very different conclusions here – *and produce equally good answers!* What matters is your evaluation of the sources, your use of your own knowledge and how you use both of these to weigh up the interpretation and make a judgement about it.

8.5 Source enquiry skills: further practice

Source D suggests that problems with Simpson's discovery of chloroform prevented it from being seen as a major advance in surgery. How far do you agree with this interpretation? Explain your answer, using your own knowledge, Sources A, B, C and D, and any other sources you find helpful [Only Sources A, B, C and D are provided in this example.]

Start by analysing the question.

- What topic knowledge do you need?
  Evidence about the importance of Simpson's discovery.
- What does the question want you to do?
  Reach a judgement about the extent to which the public viewed Simpson's discovery as a major advance in surgery.
- How do you do it?
  Select evidence from the sources and your own knowledge to weigh up the arguments for there being little public support or a lot of public support and reach a balanced judgement.

Source B: From an article in the medical journal *The Lancet,* 1853.

A very strange rumour has been spread that her Majesty, Queen Victoria, during her last childbirth, used chloroform, something which has caused death in a considerable number of cases. In several of these cases, healthy people died, and these catastrophes were clearly due to the poisonous effect of chloroform, and to that cause alone….We know that a huge amount of agony is avoided through chloroform but its unnecessary use should not be suggested, especially as the actions of royalty are quickly copied by many people.

Source C: From the Manchester Courier and Lancashire General Advertiser newspaper, 4th October 1865.

The Discoverer of Chloroform

The recent proposal to erect a statue in honour of Dr. Simpson, as the discoverer of chloroform, has given rise to some comments in the French journals, which state that, although Dr. Simpson was the first to use chloroform as an anaesthetic in surgical operations, the substance itself was discovered by M. Soubeiran, professor at the Paris School of Medicine… These experiments were made in 1831, and Dr. Simpson did not introduce chloroform as a substitute for sulphuric ether till 1847, a year after M. Floures [another French scientist] had discovered its stupefying effects on animals.

Source A: Charles Darwin's description of an operation in the early 19th century, before the use of anaesthetics.

I attended the operating theatre and saw two very bad operations… but I rushed away before they were completed. Nor did I ever attend again, for hardly any inducement would have been strong enough to make me do so; this being long before the blessed days of chloroform. The two cases fairly haunted me for many a long year.

Source D: An illustration showing the death of Hannah Greener in 1848. There was a great deal of public opposition to anaesthetics after her death, which happened after she was given chloroform during an operation to remove a toenail.

Mark your answers

The mark scheme is divided into levels and within each level there are also an additional three marks on top for spelling, punctuation and grammar.

- Basic answers give a statement that supports or opposes the interpretation, but do not support this with evidence from the sources or own knowledge. A basic answer may also take points from the sources, without linking them to an argument.
- Good answers give a judgement that agrees with the interpretation or disagrees with it, and make links to relevant details from the source **or** from own knowledge.
- Better answers explore the source evidence to make a case for or against the interpretation, but the argument may be somewhat one-sided – only one side of the argument is really explored properly.
- Excellent answers consider the evidence for and against the interpretation in a balanced way and come to an overall conclusion. They will also use own knowledge. To do really well, the answer needs to consider the strength of the evidence from the sources provided: e.g. how reliable they are.

SPaG

There are three extra marks available for really good spelling, punctuation and grammar. Answers need to be accurate all the way through, the arguments need to be clear to understand and specialist terms should be used in the right place and in the right way.

Activities

1 Read the two sample answers and decide what level you would give them.

2 Check the comments about these two answers.

3 Now write your own answer to this question and mark yourself.

Answer A

Simpson made a very great contribution to the advances of surgery because he discovered chloroform. He wanted to find a replacement for ether and invited some friends to join him in testing chemicals. When his wife found them all unconscious, he realised that chloroform was a good anaesthetic. Lots of people were opposed to the use of chloroform, especially in childbirth, because in the bible God said women will have pain in childbirth so they felt this was going against God's will. Some surgeons also opposed it because they felt patients who were awake and feeling pain were less likely to die during an operation than someone who was unconscious. The use of chloroform became very popular after Queen Victoria used it for the birth of her child. She called it 'the blessed chloroform' and after that many people accepted it. Simpson was knighted for his services to medicine.

Answer B

Although Source D shows one event in the history of chloroform being used which did make people very concerned, it is wrong to say that therefore Simpson's discovery of chloroform was not a great advance. Source A clearly explains how many people felt about the discovery of chloroform – Darwin called it 'blessed' because of how terrible surgery was before chloroform was discovered by Simpson. The event shown in Source D is also from 1848. By 1853, Queen Victoria used chloroform when she was having her eighth baby (Prince Leopold). So, in conclusion, although the death of Hannah Greener did cause public outcry about chloroform's safety, it was not long until people recognised what a great advance it really was.

Comments

Answer A provides a lot of detail about Simpson and anaesthetics but does not link this to the question or provide evidence from the sources provided. So, despite all the details, this is a basic answer only.

Answer B is much better because it engages with the question. It makes a strong argument to counter the interpretation that chloroform was not seen as a major advance in surgery and uses relevant evidence from some of the sources, plus the student's own knowledge. However, because the answer only really considers one side of the argument, it would only be a better answer. The student could have evaluated more sources for the evidence they provide in support of the interpretation.

Both answers use correct spelling and punctuation. Their arguments are clearly expressed and there is good use of specialist terms such as 'anaesthetic'.

The transformation of surgery c1845–c1918: summary

| 1840 | 1850 | 1860 | 1870 | 1880 | 1890 | 1900 | 1910 | 1920 |

Dealing with pain

Problems of pain, infection and blood loss meant that surgery was a last resort as the death rate was high

"Black Period" of surgery. Anaesthetics led to longer operations, but continued problems of blood loss and infections led to high death rates.

1844 Horace Wells uses nitrous oxide as an anaesthetic during tooth extractions

1846 Liston uses ether as an anaesthetic

1847 Simpson uses chloroform as an anaesthetic

1848 first death as a result of use of chloroform

1853 Queen Victoria uses chloroform during childbirth

1905 Novocaine used as an anaesthetic

Dealing with infection

Aseptic techniques replace antiseptic

1867 Lister uses carbolic acid as an antiseptic

1877 Lister publicises methods

1878 Koch develops steam sterilizer

Dealing with blood loss

Blood loss can only be controlled. Doctors use cautery and ligatures and keep operations short

1901 Landsteiner identifies blood groups

1915 Lewisohn uses sodium citrate to stop blood from clotting

1916 Rous and Turner use citrate glucose solution to store blood for longer

1917 first blood depot established for the Battle of Cambrai

Factors influencing these developments

First World War [1914-1918]

1853 Alexander Wood invents hypodermic needle

1861 Pasteur publishes Germ Theory

1895 Roentgen discovers X-rays

1916 Gillies sets up plastic surgery unit at Aldershot

Introduction

This unit tests your understanding of how to use sources in a historical enquiry. Because it is important to understand what a source is about and to know about a source's reliability and how representative it is of the situation at the time, this work has been set in the context of a period of dramatic changes in surgery. Your knowledge of this topic will help you to evaluate and use the sources, but you are not expected to have any other knowledge of medicine at this time.

In the exam you will have 1 hour and 15 minutes to answer five questions. You do not have any choice in the questions in this exam so you need to make sure you have covered the whole unit and you are prepared for the sorts of question that are likely to be asked.

All the questions will focus on evidence skills, but you will need your knowledge of the topic to help you understand and evaluate the sources. For all except question 1, you must use the sources and your own knowledge in your answer.

Checklist (factual details)

The key factual themes throughout this unit are:
- dealing with pain, for example the importance of the discovery of anaesthetics, the problems in using ether and chloroform, the work of Simpson, and changing attitudes towards anaesthetics
- dealing with infection, for example Lister's use of carbolic acid, the reactions of other doctors, and the development of antiseptic and aseptic conditions
- dealing with blood loss and storage, for example the use of ligatures and the importance of the development of transfusions and techniques to store blood

- the role of factors in these developments, for example showing the importance of scientific knowledge and technology, communications, changing attitudes, etc
- the extent of progress within surgery, for example weighing up the advantages of anaesthetics against the problems caused when surgeons began to do more internal operations without a proper understanding of germs and the need for antiseptics.

Support activity

You may find it helpful to do a series of ideas maps like this one:

Attitudes towards pain relief	Ether	Problems with anaesthetics

Dealing with pain

Chloroform	Problem of pain before anaesthetics

Student tip

I found it helpful to write out summaries using different colours to show the advantages and problems of each development.

Checklist (evidence skills)

The questions in this unit test five key areas:

- **inference** – your ability to work things out from the source, for example what you can work out about a situation, the attitude of the author, the message of a cartoon, the purpose of a speech

- **purpose** – how the content of a source has been treated or selected in order to create a particular effect or message

- **source comprehension** – understanding the information a source is providing and using this information in a relevant way to answer a particular question

- **source reliability** – the use of various checks to see how reliable a source is

- **reaching a judgement** – weighing up all the evidence on an issue in order to come to a thoughtful and supported conclusion.

examzone
Watch out!

Students often remember to give both sides of an issue but they do not weigh them up properly in order to reach a conclusion. Make it clear how you are reaching your judgement.

- Are you deciding which source is more reliable by looking at how representative it is; its origins, nature and intention; how selective it is in its focus; which source tells you about the overall context; or which source gives you insight into people's attitudes?

- When you make a judgement about how important something has been, do you decide on the basis of how much it changed the situation, how quickly it became widely accepted, or how many of the problems it solved?

Support activity

Weigh up all the different elements of the source as you decide how reliable it is:

Content – how helpful is it?	Source A	Source B
Content – is there added value/weakness due to details, e.g. eyewitnesses or 'loaded' language?		
Origins – any added value/weakness due to the author's involvement? Was the account written long after the event?		
Purpose – is there any added value/weakness due to the purpose or intended audience?		
Selection – are there any signs of deliberately selecting/missing out key information? How representative is this source?		

How important was the discovery of antiseptics?

Support activity

You may find it helpful to think in terms of weighing sources on scales or a seesaw.

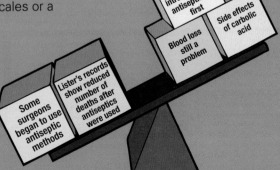

How important was the discovery of antiseptics?

examzone

Build better answers

What can you learn from Source A about how injuries in the First World War required new approaches to surgery? (6 marks)

Source A: Four photographs recording the facial reconstruction of a solider wounded during the Battle of the Somme in July 1916.

Student answer

The First World War meant really horrific injuries from shells and shrapnel. Plastic surgery was how they fixed these injuries.

Comments

This answer makes two valid inferences but it doesn't link those inferences to details from the source. You do not need to use your own knowledge in this question: work from what the source tells you.

Improved student answer

The source shows a horrific injury to the soldier's cheek and demonstrates how this injury was gradually repaired. The third and fourth photos show patches of new skin on the soldier's face. These look like skin grafts. It is likely that surgeons hadn't seen wounds like this before the First World War. So this skin grafting technique was a new technique to treat all the wounded soldiers like this one.

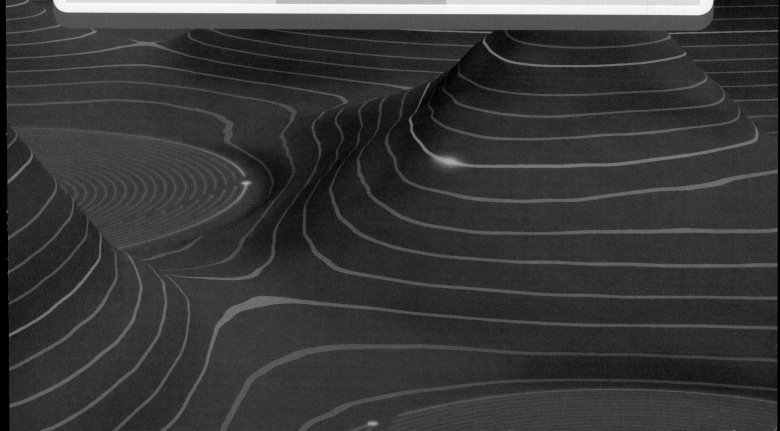

examzone

What was the purpose of this representation? Explain your answer, using Source B and your own knowledge. (8 marks)

Source B: Snow's chloroform inhaler, invented in 1848.

Student answer

It is to show how the inhaler works and how it should be fitted to a patient. The inhaler has been 'cut away' to show the details of how it works, so the picture was probably to show doctors how to use it rather than for patients.

Comments

This has made valid comments about the purpose of the representation, which have been linked to details from the representation. The student hasn't really used anything that isn't in the source, though, so they haven't used their own knowledge. To do really well, you must make very clear use of your own knowledge of the historical context as well as details from the source.

Improved student answer

The representation is designed to show doctors how to operate this chloroform inhaler. This is shown by the precise, technical style of drawing which includes a 'cut away' section of the inhaler to demonstrate the way it works. The fact that the representation shows a young woman using the inhaler may be significant too. John Snow, the designer of the inhaler, is famous for having administered chloroform to help women with the pain of childbirth.

Why was there opposition to the use of chloroform as an anaesthetic? Explain your answer, using Source C and your own knowledge. (10 marks)

Source C: From a speech by James Simpson to a meeting of doctors in Edinburgh in 1847.

In years to come people will look back with sorrow at our reactions to anaesthetics. They will be amazed at the idea of humane men saying they prefer operating on patients who are conscious instead of anaesthetised, and that the fearful agonies of an operation should be endured quietly.

Student answer

The reason that some surgeons opposed the use of chloroform was that some of them thought it was better if the patients were not unconscious during the operation but were conscious instead.

Comments

This answer has used relevant information in the source but has not really used this information to explain anything. Nor has the student used any of their own knowledge of this topic in their answer. For example, a better answer would have used own knowledge to explain why some surgeons thought it was better to operate on people while they were conscious.

Improved student answer

One reason for opposition to the use of chloroform in operations was that, as the source says, some surgeons thought it was better if the patients were not unconscious during the operation. This was because of concerns that it was easier for a patient to die during the operation if they had been made unconscious than if they were awake and struggling. There were, in fact, a number of high-profile cases soon after the introduction of chloroform in which patients did die – for example the death of Hannah Greener in 1848: the year after this speech was made. Other reasons for opposition included religious concerns: the Bible said that women's pain from childbirth was a punishment for Eve's sin in the Garden of Eden and therefore using chloroform was going against God's wishes.

How reliable are sources C and D as evidence of the impact of the discovery of x-rays? Explain your answer using sources C and D and your own knowledge. (10 marks)

Source C: From an article written in the Western Journal of Medicine in 1996 to celebrate 100 years since the discovery of x-rays by Röntgen.

The day after Röntgen's announcement, Dr J.R. Ratcliffe in Birmingham, England, produced a radiograph [x-ray] of his hand after he had pushed a sterilized needle under the skin of his palm. The film, of course, demonstrated the location of the needle. The following night, a woman came to Queen's Hospital in Birmingham with a needle embedded in her hand. Ratcliffe and colleague Hall-Edwards made a radiographic image of her hand… They gave the print to the patient, who took it to her surgeon the next morning. The surgeon used the photograph as a guide in removing the needle.

Source D: A poem printed in a magazine called *Electrical Review* in 1896.

X-actly so!
The Roentgen Rays, the Roentgen Rays,
What is this craze?
The town's ablaze
With the new phase
Of X-ray's ways.

I'm full of daze,
Shock and amaze;
For nowadays
I hear they'll gaze
Thro' cloak and gown – and even stays*,
These naughty, naughty Roentgen Rays.

*'stays' were part of a woman's corset: equivalent to a bra today.

Student answer

Source C comes from an authoritative source because it is from an academic journal. This means we can trust the account it gives of how quickly some surgeons began to use x-rays. But it does not give a comprehensive account of the impact of the discovery. We do not know if other surgeons also started using x-rays immediately, too. Source D is not reliable because it is just a poem about how x-rays can see through clothes and doesn't say anything about surgery.

Comments

This answer is good on Source C and its evaluation of its authorship. The student could make it even better by using their own knowledge to say if the source's information is correct or not. The student should have put more effort into their analysis of Source D, considering how representative and reliable it could be in context of their own knowledge.

Improved student answer

Röntgen's discovery of x-rays was immediately taken up by surgeons in Britain: within a year, x-rays had been used to locate shrapnel in wounds and kidney stones. Although Source C is not comprehensive – it describes only one account – it is therefore a reliable source in indicating the speed of the impact on surgery.

Source C comes from an authoritative source because it is from an academic journal. This means we can trust the account it gives of how quickly some surgeons began to use x-rays.

While Source C was written 100 years after the discovery of x-rays, Source D is representative of the views of the time as it comes from 1896. There was a 'craze' about x-rays and Source D is a reliable source for this and for what made people most fascinated – the idea of being able to see through solid objects – including underwear! It is not possible from Source D to know whether public opinion about x-rays meant that people were willing or not willing to be treated with x-rays. Source D also does not tell us about how surgeons viewed x-rays.

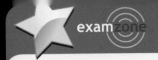
Source C suggests that surgery in the 19th century improved significantly with the use of anaesthetics. How far do you agree with this interpretation? Explain your answer, using your own knowledge, Sources C, D and E, and any other sources you find helpful. (16 marks + 3 marks for SPaG)

Source C: A comment from Dr Wilkinson, the keeper of the historical documents for the Royal Society of Anaesthetists.

On 19 December 1846 in Dumfries ether was used to amputate the leg of a patient who had been run over by a cart; it is believed that the patient died. Two days later, at University College Hospital, London, Robert Liston amputated the leg of a chauffeur, Frederick Churchill, while a medical student called William Squires gave an ether anaesthetic to the patient.

It is difficult to understand today how major this advance was. Before this, surgery was a terrifying last resort in a final attempt to save life. Few operations were possible and the key to being a successful surgeon was speed. Most patients were held or strapped down – some would mercifully faint from their agony – many died, either on the table or shortly afterwards. The suffering was intense.

Source D: From Simpson's *Account of an Anaesthetic Agent* published in 1847.

From the time when I first saw ether being successfully used, I was convinced that we would find other substances which could achieve the same effects. I have talked about this with various professional friends, who know more about chemistry than I do, and I have had different drugs manufactured for me by the local chemist. The one which I have found most effective is chloroform and I have tried it on more than thirty individuals.

The advantage of using chloroform rather than ether is that less chloroform is needed to achieve the same state of unconsciousness; it works more quickly than ether; it is more agreeable to inhale and the odour does not remain on someone's breath or clothes.

Source E: An operation at the Metropolitan Hospital in 1896 showing the use of anaesthetics.

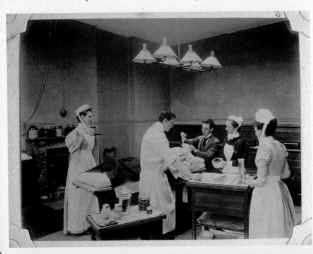

Student answer

Surgery before anaesthetics was very painful and therefore surgeons aimed to be as quick as possible. This meant that only simple operations could be done and surgeons did not dare risk doing surgery inside the chest or the stomach. The discovery of ether as an anaesthetic was a very important step in progress in surgery because the patient was not in pain and was not struggling. This meant the surgeon could take longer and do a more careful job.

The use of ether caused some problems because it tended to irritate the lungs of the patient and make them cough during the operation. It also made people vomit sometimes and was highly flammable. Therefore James Simpson searched for a better anaesthetic and discovered chloroform.

Although some people opposed the use of anaesthetics, particularly for childbirth, most people quickly accepted it, and when Queen Victoria used chloroform for the birth of her eighth child it was seen to be accepted.

However, chloroform was not completely safe and it was difficult to measure the dose, so some people died, such as Hannah Greener during an operation to remove her toenail. There were also other problems because anaesthetics encouraged surgeons to try out more complex operations and, when they put their dirty hands and instruments into the open wound, they were actually making infection worse. For this reason, the death rate rose. Furthermore, there was still the problem of blood loss – which became more of a problem if the operations went on for too long or went deeper into the body.

So, I would agree with the interpretation that anaesthetics were a significant breakthrough and did lead to progress in surgery in the 19th century. However, in my view, the real improvements did not come until the problems of infection and blood loss had also been dealt with, so anaesthetics alone did not lead to truly significant improvements. on for too long or went deeper into the body.

Comments

This answer shows excellent understanding of the issue, and excellent knowledge is used to back up the comments. The student reaches a balanced judgement on how far they agree with the interpretation, weighing up the problems with operations before anaesthetics, the significance of the discovery of anaesthetics, problems and improvements in anaesthetics against the remaining problems of infection and blood loss. HOWEVER, the answer does not use evidence from the sources to back up this excellent evaluation and that means it doesn't reach its full potential. The student's spelling, punctuation and grammar is good but fairly basic.

Improved student answer

Surgery before anaesthetics was very painful and therefore surgeons aimed to be as quick as possible, as evidenced in Source C. This meant that only simple operations could be done and surgeons did not dare risk doing surgery inside the chest or stomach. The use of anaesthetics helped to relieve pain, which was a major problem in surgery in the 19th century and therefore it was a significant improvement. Surgeons now felt they could develop their skill further rather than having to act as quickly as possible and surgery seemed less like butchery. Source C stresses this when it says that, pre-anaesthetics, 'surgery was a terrifying last resort'. However, the use of ether caused some problems because it tended to irritate the lungs of the patient and make them cough during the operation. It also made people vomit sometimes and was highly flammable. Therefore, James Simpson searched for a better anaesthetic and discovered chloroform, and the benefits of chloroform are described in Source B. The fact that it was used in many hospitals is shown in Source E, but some people opposed the use of anaesthetics, particularly for childbirth. Nevertheless, most people quickly accepted it and, when Queen Victoria used chloroform for the birth of her eighth child, it was seen to be accepted. However, chloroform was not completely safe and it was difficult to measure the dose, so some people died, such as Hannah Greener during an operation to remove her toenail. Anaesthetics encouraged surgeons to try out more complex operations and, when they put their dirty hands and instruments into the open wound, they were actually making infection worse. For this reason the death rate rose. Furthermore, there was still the problem of blood loss – which became more of a problem if the operations went on for too long or went deeper into the body. So, I would agree with the interpretation that anaesthetics were a significant breakthrough and did lead to progress in surgery in the 19th century. However, in my view, the real improvements did not come until the problems of infection and blood loss had also been dealt with, so anaesthetics alone did not lead to truly significant improvements.

Welcome to examzone

Revising for your exams can be a daunting prospect. In this part of the book we'll take you through the best way of revising for your exams, step by step, to ensure you answer the questions to the best of your ability.

Zone In!

Have you ever become so absorbed in a task that suddenly it feels entirely natural and easy to perform? This is a feeling familiar to many athletes and performers. They work hard to recreate it in competition in order to do their very best. It's a feeling of being 'in the zone', and if you can achieve that same feeling in an examination, the chances are you'll perform brilliantly.

The good news is that you can get 'in the zone' by taking some simple steps in advance of the exam. Here are our top tips.

UNDERSTAND IT

Make sure you understand the exam process and what revision you need to do. This will give you confidence and also help you to get things into proportion. These pages are a good place to find some starting pointers for performing well in exams.

BUILD CONFIDENCE

Use your revision time not only to revise content, but also to build your confidence in readiness for tackling the examination. For example, try tackling a short sequence of easy tasks in record time.

DEAL WITH DISTRACTIONS

Think about the issues in your life that may interfere with revision. Write them all down. Then think about how you can deal with each so they don't affect your revision.

FRIENDS AND FAMILY

Make sure that your friends and family know when you want to revise. Even share your revision plan with them. Learn to control your times with them, so you don't get distracted. This means you can have better quality time with them when you aren't revising, because you aren't worrying about what you ought to be doing.

DIET AND EXERCISE

Make sure you eat sensibly and exercise as well! If your body is not in the right state, how can your mind be? A substantial breakfast will set you up for the day, and a light evening meal will keep your energy levels high. Also, make sure you drink plenty of water while revising, and during the exam. Even at rest, your brain uses up about 30% of your energy and fluid intake to work effectively!

COMPARTMENTALISE

You might not be able to deal with all the issues that can distract you. For example, you may be worried about a friend who is ill, or just be afraid of the exam. In this case, there is still a useful technique you can use. Put all of these worries into an imagined box in your mind at the start of your revision (or in the exam) and mentally lock it. Only open it again at the end of your revision session (or exam).

Planning Zone

The key to success in exams and revision often lies in good planning. Knowing **what** you need to do and **when** you need to do it is your best path to a stress-free experience. Here are some top tips in creating a great personal revision plan.

First of all, **know your strengths and weaknesses**.

Go through each topic making a list of how well you think you know the topic. Use your mock examination results and/or any other test results that are available as a check on your self-assessment. This will help you to plan your personal revision effectively, putting extra time into your weaker areas.

Next, *create your plan!*

Remember to make time for considering how topics interrelate.

For example, in History you will be expected to know not just the date when an event happened, but why it happened, how important it was, and how one event relates to another.

The specification quite clearly states when you are expected to be able to link one topic to another so plan this into your revision sessions.

You will be tested on this in the exam and you can do well by showing your ability to do this.

Finally, *follow the plan!*

You can use the revision sections in the following pages to kick-start your revision.

149

MAY

SUNDAY	MONDAY	TUES
29	30	1

Be realistic about how much time you can devote to your revision, but also make sure you put in enough time. Give yourself regular breaks or different activities to give your life some variance. Revision need not be a prison sentence!

Find out your exam dates. Go to the Edexcel website to find all final exam dates, and check with your teacher.

iew Sectio
complete ty
ractice exa
question

Chunk your revision in each subject down into smaller sections. This will make it more manageable and less daunting.

Draw up a list of all the dates from the start of your revision right through to your exams.

13

7

8

Review Sectio
Complete three
practice exam

20

Review Sectio
Try the Keywor
Quiz again

Make sure you allow time for assessing your progress against your initial self-assessment. Measuring progress will allow you to see and be encouraged by your improvement. These little victories will build your confidence.

22

EXAM DAY!

27

28

29

Don't Panic Zone

As you get close to completing your revision, the Big Day will be getting nearer and nearer. Many students find this the most stressful time and tend to go into panic mode, either working long hours without really giving their brains a chance to absorb information or giving up and staring blankly at the wall.

Panicking simply makes your brain seize up and you find that information and thoughts simply cannot flow naturally. You become distracted and anxious, and things seem worse than they are. Many students build the exams up into more than they are. Remember: the exams are not trying to catch you out! If you have studied the course, there will be no surprises on the exam paper!

Student tip

I know how silly it is to panic, especially if you've done the work and know your stuff. I was asked by a teacher to produce a report on a project I'd done, and I panicked so much I spent the whole afternoon crying and worrying. I asked other people for help, but they were panicking too. In the end, I calmed down and looked at the task again. It turned out to be quite straightforward and, in the end, I got my report finished first and it was the best of them all!

In the exam you don't have much time, so you can't waste it by panicking. The best way to control panic is simply to do what you have to do. Think carefully for a few minutes, then start writing and, as you do, the panic will drain away.

Don't panic

ExamZone

Make sure you know in which order you are sitting your exams and prepare for each accordingly – check with your teacher if you're not sure. They are likely to be about a week apart, so make sure you allow plenty of revision time for each before your first exam.

For the **Medicine and public health in Britain c50AD to the present day** paper, you will have an hour and a quarter for the exam, and in that time you have to answer five questions. You need to answer Questions 1, 2 and 3. Then you must choose to answer either Question 4 or Question 5, and then choose to answer one question from Questions 6 and 7.

For the **Transformation of surgery** paper, you will have an hour and a quarter and in that time you have to answer five questions. There are no choices for this exam.

Each question on each paper is worth a different number of marks and it is important that you use your time effectively. Don't waste precious time on a 6-mark question that might then leave you with too little time to spend on a question which is worth 16 marks – plus an extra 3 for SPaG!

Understand it. Now is a good opportunity to ask your teacher about anything you are not sure of here.

Print your surname here, and your other names afterwards. This is an additional safeguard to ensure that the exam board awards the marks to the right candidate.

Here you fill in the school's exam number.

Ensure that you understand exactly how long the examination will last, and plan your time accordingly.

Note that the quality of your written communication will also be marked. Take particular care to present your thoughts and work at the highest standard you can.

Here you fill in your personal exam number. Take care when writing it down because the number is important to the exam board when writing your score.

In this box, the examiner will write the total marks you have achieved in the exam paper.

Make sure that you understand exactly which questions from which sections you should attempt.

Don't feel that you have to fill the answer space provided. Everybody's handwriting varies, so a long answer from you may take up as much space as a short answer from someone else.

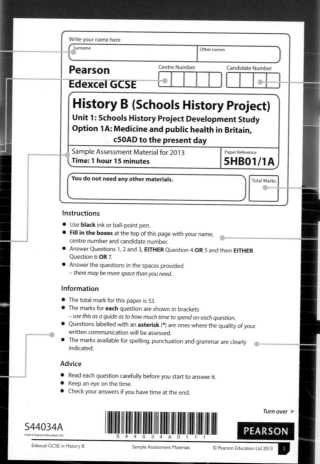

Write your name here

Surname

Other names

Pearson
Edexcel GCSE

Centre Number

Candidate Number

History B (Schools History Project)

Unit 1: Schools History Project Development Study
Option 1A: Medicine and public health in Britain, c50AD to the present day

Sample Assessment Material for 2013
Time: 1 hour 15 minutes

Paper Reference
5HB01/1A

You do not need any other materials.

Total Marks

Instructions

● Use **black** ink or ball-point pen.
● **Fill in the boxes** at the top of this page with your name, centre number and candidate number.
● Answer Questions 1, 2 and 3, **EITHER** Question 4 **OR** 5 and then **EITHER** Question 6 **OR** 7.
● Answer the questions in the spaces provided
– there may be more space than you need.

Information

● The total mark for this paper is 53.
● The marks for **each** question are shown in brackets
– use this as a guide as to how much time to spend on each question.
● Questions labelled with an **asterisk** (*) are ones where the quality of your written communication will be assessed.
● The marks available for spelling, punctuation and grammar are clearly indicated.

Advice

● Read each question carefully before you start to answer it.
● Keep an eye on the time.
● Check your answers if you have time at the end.

Turn over ▶

S44034A
©2013 Pearson Education Ltd.

Edexcel GCSE in History B   Sample Assessment Materials   © Pearson Education Ltd 2013   3

PEARSON

Understanding the language of the exam paper

Describe	You need to give a concise and organised account.
Explain how/why	You need to show that you understand the key ideas about how and why developments happened in the history of medicine. The more detail you can give, the better.
How useful...? How reliable...?	These questions involve source evaluation skills – look for clues that tell you about origins, intention, nature, selection...
How far...	Questions that ask 'How far do you agree...' with an interpretation are looking for you to consider different sides and come up with a balanced judgement.

This section provides answers to the most common questions students have about what happens after they complete their exams. For more information, visit www.examzone.co.uk.

About your grades

Whether you've done better than, worse than, or just as you expected, your grades are the final measure of your performance on your course and in the exams. On this page we explain some of the information that appears on your results slip and tell you what to do if you think something is wrong. We answer the most common questions about grades and look at some of the options facing you.

When will my results be published?

Results for GCSE examinations are issued on the third Thursday in August.

Can I get my results online?

Visit www.resultsplusdirect.co.uk, where you will find detailed student results information including the 'Edexcel Gradeometer' which demonstrates how close you were to the nearest grade boundary.

I haven't done as well as I expected. What can I do now?

First of all, talk to your teacher. After all the teaching that you have had, and the tests and internal examinations you have done, he/she is the person who best knows what grade you are capable of achieving. Take your results slip to your subject teacher, and go through the information on it in detail. If you both think that there is something wrong with the result, the school or college can apply to see your completed examination paper and then, if necessary, ask for a re-mark immediately.

Can I have a re-mark of my examination paper?

Yes, this is possible, but remember only your school or college can apply for a re-mark, not you or your parents/carers. First of all you should consider carefully whether or not to ask your school or college to make a request for a re-mark. It is worth knowing that very few re-marks result in a change to a grade, simply because a re-mark request has shown that the original marking was accurate. Check the closing date for re-marking requests with your Examinations Officer

Bear in mind that there is no guarantee that your grades will go up if your papers are re-marked. The original mark can be confirmed or lowered, as well as raised, as a result of a re-mark.

Glossary

This Glossary contains all the key word definitions, plus some other terms used in the book that may be unfamiliar to you. When appropriate the definitions are particularly directed to the period being studied.

Ague – An old term for illnesses that involve fever and fits of shivering.

Almshouse – A house founded by charity, offering accommodation for the poor.

Alternative medicine – Medicine that uses herbs and other natural remedies, as well as therapies such as acupuncture, instead of drugs.

Amputation – The cutting off of a limb – for example, an arm or a leg – from the body.

Anaesthetic – A substance that affects your nervous system so that you are less aware of sensation and don't feel pain.

Anatomy – The structure of the body, for example bones, nerves, muscles.

Antibiotics – Drugs that stop infections caused by **bacteria**.

Antibodies – Special cells created by the body to fight infection and disease.

Antiseptic – Something that fights against **sepsis** and the **microbes** that create infection.

Apothecary – A person who made medicines and ointments using ingredients such as herbs and spices.

Appendix – A tube-shaped sac attached to the large intestine; appendicitis occurs when it is inflamed.

Artery – A blood vessel that carries blood from the heart to all parts of the body.

Aseptic – Sterile; free from the **microbes** that cause infection.

Astrology – The study of the stars and planets and how they are thought to affect humans and nature.

Asylum – An old type of hospital for those who were mentally ill.

Bacteria – Micro-organisms that live in soil, water, plants and animals and that can cause diseases.

Bile – A thick, bitter fluid produced by the liver; a liquid once thought to be one of the **Four Humours**.

Black Death – A highly infectious disease that spread throughout Europe in the mid-14th century.

Bloodletting – The drawing of blood from a patient by a doctor.

Body snatcher – A person who used to obtain dead bodies illegally and sell them to medical schools for dissection.

By-law – A law made by a town's local authority that affects only that town.

Cautery – The use of heat to seal blood vessels and stop bleeding.

Cesspit – A pit for the disposal of liquid waste and sewage, for homes that aren't connected to a **sewer**.

Chamber pot – A 'potty' that was kept in a room or chamber, for people who needed the toilet and did not go to the outside privy or **latrine**.

Chromosomes – Thread-like structures found in most living cells that carry **genetic** information.

Church, The – The international organisation of all Christian believers.

Cloning – Using cells from one organism to make another identical organism.

Consultant – A doctor specialising in a specific disease or part of the body; usually based in hospital and seeing patients referred by a **general practitioner (GP)**.

Crystallography – Using radiation to take a high-power X-ray photograph.

Curare – A poison obtained from South American plants and used as an **anaesthetic**.

Diagnosis – Identifying an illness by examining the symptoms.

Dialysis – Removal of impurities from the blood by a kidney machine.

Dissection – Cutting open a body to examine its internal structure.

DNA – The abbreviation for deoxyribonucleic acid, which contains the genetic instructions for every cell in your body.

Druid – A priest or magician of the ancient Celtic religion.

Endoscope – An instrument with a tiny camera on the end that can be used to look at the internal parts of the body.

Epidemic – A severe outbreak of an infectious disease.

Ethics – A set of moral principles followed by members of a profession, such as medical ethics.

Flagellants – People who whip themselves as a punishment and to show God that they are sorry.

Folk remedies – Traditional remedies practised by ordinary people, not doctors, and passed down through history, often by word of mouth.

Four Humours – A theory that developed in Ancient Greece to explain illness.

Gall bladder – The sac attached to the liver that stores **bile**.

Gangrene – Occurs when body tissue dies, which can be caused by infection or bad circulation.

General practitioner (GP) – A doctor who works in a practice dealing directly with the public.

Genetics – The study of genes and inherited characteristics.

Herbals – Books containing descriptions of plants used in herbal medicine.

Hereditary – Passed on from one generation of a family to another.

Hygiene – Conditions or practices, especially cleanliness, that maintain health and prevent disease.

Hypnotism – Putting a person into a trance-like state that is like sleep, but in which the person readily accepts suggestions and acts on them.

Glossary

Immunisation – Making immune to infection, usually by **vaccination**.

Industrial – Connected to industry and manufacturing.

Industrial revolution – The period c1750–c1900 when there were rapid changes in the way work and industry were organised.

Inoculation – A way of giving a patient a mild dose of an illness so that the body builds up its immunity.

Journal – (1) An account that is written up at regular intervals, like a diary – this is a personal and private source. (2) A published set of articles (like an academic magazine), for example *The Lancet* is a respected medical journal containing articles by doctors and researchers.

Laissez-faire – The idea that government should not interfere too much with industry and private business.

Latrine – A toilet, especially a communal one, often in an army camp, for example.

Leech – A blood-sucking worm used to draw blood from a patient; also an old name for a **physician**.

Ligature – A thread tied around a blood vessel to stop bleeding.

Magic bullet – A chemical drug that kills the **microbes** causing a specific disease without harming the rest of the body.

Malaria – 'Bad air'; people used to believe that malaria was a fever caused by poisonous air arising from marshes. The illness is now known to be caused by mosquitoes.

Medieval – A name for the 'Middle Ages', the period between the Ancient World (which ended when the Romans left Britain) and the Renaissance of the 16th and 17th centuries.

Miasma – The theory that disease is caused by poisonous vapours in the air.

Microbes – Micro-organisms, especially **bacteria** causing disease.

Midwife – A woman, or nowadays also a man, who assists women in childbirth.

National Health Service (NHS) – An organisation set up by the government in 1948 to give free health care to all.

Obesity – The state of being grossly fat or overweight.

Opium – An addictive drug prepared from the juice of the poppy, which can be used to ease pain.

Patent medicine – A mixture that has been created by one person or company and is sold under a particular brand name.

Pharmaceutical industry – The business of manufacturing medicinal drugs, prescribed by a doctor or sold by a chemist.

Pharmacy – A business selling medical drugs; a chemist's.

Physician – A trained doctor.

Physiology – The way organs function within the body, for example the work of the heart, liver and kidneys.

Plastic surgery – Surgery carried out in order to change the appearance of the patient.

Prescription charges – Payment for medicine that has been prescribed by a doctor.

Prosthetic limb – Artificial arm or leg, often made from metal and plastic.

Public health – The standard of living conditions and general health of the people.

Public health provision – Health provision for the whole community, such as the provision of fresh water, **sewers** and the availability of health care.

Purging – Getting rid of bad or excess humours by making someone sick or by making them have diarrhoea.

Quarantine – The situation where someone who may have an infectious disease is isolated from other people to try to prevent the disease spreading; often the whole family is isolated.

Radiotherapy – The use of radiation in medicine, often to attack cancer.

Reformation – A period of challenges and divisions within the Christian Church.

Renaissance – A period in the 16th and 17th centuries when people thought they were reviving Ancient Greek and Ancient Roman culture but also made new discoveries.

Royal Society – A group set up in 1660 to enable educated people to discuss scientific ideas.

Sanitation – Measures for the promotion of health and prevention of disease, especially the provision of drainage and **sewers**.

Sepsis – A condition in which harmful **bacteria** affect the flesh, normally leading to infection and decaying flesh.

Sewer – An underground system for removing liquid waste (sewage).

Society – The way a group of people links together in some common ways.

Spontaneous generation – The idea that rubbish or decaying material creates **microbes**.

Superbugs – **Bacteria** that have become resistant to **antibiotics**.

Supernatural – Forces outside normal nature that some people believe can affect events, for example God, charms and luck, witchcraft or **astrology**.

Surgeon – Someone who deals with wounds or with treatment that involves cutting the body.

Tourniquet – Something that is tied around a part of the body to put pressure on a blood vessel and stop the loss of blood.

Transfusion – The process of giving blood from a donor to the patient.

Vaccination – A safe way of stimulating the body's immune system against a particular disease.

Vein – A blood vessel that carries blood from all parts of the body towards the heart.

Welfare State – The coordination and provision by the government of all matters affecting the health of the people.

Workhouse – An institution where people could go if they could not support themselves; they would be expected to work in return for their food and bed.

Index

In the following index, main entries of key words are given in bold type and the page number that is also in bold will lead you to a definition of the word. For all these definitions, as well as further definitions of unfamiliar words, see the Glossary on pages 156–157.